Exploring

Bowness-on-Solway Peninsular

on the 93 Bus Service

Geoffrey Hugh Lindop

Mercianotes

First published by Mercianotes 2017

Published by
Mercianotes,
Brackenrigg
Wigton,
Cumbria
CA7 5AQ

© 2017 Mercianotes

ISBN: 978-1537177199

www.mercianotes.com

Email: bowness@mercianotes.com

Exploring the

Bowness-on-Solway Peninsular

on the 93 Bus Service

Contents

Introduction

The Timetables reproduced in this book have kindly been provided by Stagecoach and are valid from 5 September 2016. The latest timetable can be found on the following websites:

http://www.cumbria.gov.uk/roads-transport/public-transport-road-safety/transport/publictransport/busserv/timetables/carlisle.asp

https://www.stagecoachbus.com/timetables
enter 93 in the *Download bus timetable PDF* search box

The journey with its items of interest is described in Part One of this book. There are two bus services, the 93 and the 93A. Both serve identical routes but the 93 goes anti-clockwise around the peninsular, while the 93 goes clockwise. This book is written based on the 93 service. For readers using the 93A, please start towards the back of the book and work forward. The items of interest are numbered, so it is easy to read the paragraphs in reverse numerical order. The timetable, which lists the appropriate page to start reading, is given on page 8.

Each chapter in Part One starts with a Journey Page. At the top and bottom of the Journey Page is the name of the bus stop and the timetable for that specific stop. Depending upon which service is used the page should be read from top to bottom (93 Service) or from bottom to top (93A Service). An arrow by the timetable confirms which. A horizontal line separates the header and footer from the rest of the page. A vertical line separates the 93 service (on the right) from the 93A service (on the left). An arrow shows which bus window to look through for the specific item of interest.

<u>Key to symbols used</u>

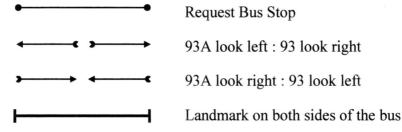

A book this size can only deal briefly with each subject but more information is available online and where appropriate the website URL is given. Readers with mobile devices can scan the QR code within the appropriate paragraph (like the one here) to quickly reach that website automatically.

There are many places to stay on the bus route to enable a more detailed appreciation of the beauty, history and wildlife of the area from the many walks. The use of the bus service enables the walker to start at one bus stop and be picked up at another, rather than the more conventional circular walk where a return to the parked car is required. The walks are described in Part Two, which should be read in conjunction with the Ordnance Survey Explorer Maps; Number 314 for the Solway Firth, and Number 315 for Carlisle. Purchase of both maps will cost £17.98. However, the Ordnance Survey will produce a custom made map centred on the 93 Bus route for £16.99 from their online shop. The website will ask for the scale, which is 1:25000 and the coordinates of the centre, which are 327000,557000. The OS website is at: https://www.ordnancesurvey.co.uk/shop/ . In Part Two of this book GPS coordinates are given for people without such maps. If neither GPS device nor Ordnance Survey map are available then reference should be made to Google Maps and search for the GPS coordinates. The satellite (aerial) view on the Google Map at that coordinate is best.

The order of telling the Peninsular story does not necessarily conform to the order of the bus routes, so Part Three provides the background to the items of interest.

Some of the walks pass through more than one nature reserve, so Part Four gives a more detailed description for the eco-tourist and Part Five completes the book with odd miscellaneous items.

Welcome to Carlisle

Our adventure starts when we board the 93 (or 93A) bus at the Carlisle Bus Station in Earls Lane, just off Lowther Street. If you have arrived in Carlisle by Bus you will already be at the bus station. But if you have arrived by train you need to make a short (500 metre) walk

The Citadel

Time to spare? Walk through the centre of the Citadel to the many shops and cafes in the pedestrianized city centre.

In a hurry? Walk to the right of the Citadel down Lowther Street. The Earls Lane Bus Station is on the right hand side of street.

Carlisle was served by several railway companies each with its own station but in 1847 they all shared a single station known as the Citadel Station - the present and only station. It was named after the Citadel, a fortified part of the medieval town, which formed part of the city wall. From here it is a short walk to the bus station. The direct route is down Lowther Street, but if you have sufficient time, it is recommended that you walk along English Street through the pedestrianized area and and enjoy the many restaurants, cafes and shops that line the route.

In a typical Victorian town or city, the prosperous dwellings were close to the slums of the poor and Carlisle was no exception. Lowther Street, English Street and Scotch street featured prosperous houses whilst a series of lanes linking them found the dwellings of the poor. In the late 1960's the Lanes, as they were collectively called, fell into disrepair and by the early 1970's were demolished to make way for a brand new shopping centre. Known as the Lanes Shopping Centre it retained the original layout of the old lanes with the addition of a new lane running north-south.

Before you begin your journey on the 93 bus, or after you have finished, I would recommend you walk down Castle Street. The magnificent Cathedral is situated here. Further down Castle Street is

The Old Town Hall

Time to Spare? Walk to the left of the Old Town Hall and turn right at The Crown and Mitre. The Cathedral, Tullie House and the Castle are down Castle Street.

Need Help? The Tourist Information Office is up the steps in the Old Town Hall.

In a hurry? Walk to the right of the Old Town Hall. Through The Lanes Shopping Mall. The public toilets are on the way to the Bus Station.

the Tullie House museum where artefacts and background information can be seen relating to topics covered in this book. Tullie House has been refurbished presenting history - both local and natural - in a modern and exciting way. Castle Street ends in an underpass giving pedestrian access to Carlisle Castle, which is also worth a visit.

On your way to the Bus Station, walk through the Lanes Shopping centre, where public toilets can be found. In the middle of the Lanes is the Public Library, where public access computers are available with fast broadband connection. The local history Librarian, Stephen White, has written an excellent book on the local railways and is responsible for keeping the local history section well stocked.

Motorists can park close to the bus station. There are two car parks along Lowther Street. The Lane Multi-storey is part of the Shopping Mall and a 'Pay and Display' open air car park is on the other side of the road.

The Lanes Shopping Centre

Part 1 - Enjoy the Ride

93A Service

Bus Stop	Time	Time	See page
Carlisle Bus Station	06:35	09:10	48
West Tower Street	06:38	09:13	48
Moorhouse	06:52	09:27	46
Thurstonfield	06:55	09:30	46
Kirkbampton	06:58	09:33	44
Kirkbride	07:09	09:44	40
Anthorn	07:20	09:55	36
Cardurnock		10:00	30
Bowness on Solway	07:34	10:12	28
Port Carlisle	07:38	10:16	26
Glasson	07:43	10:21	22
Drumburgh	07:47	10:25	18
Dykesfield	07:52	10:30	16
Burgh by Sands	07:55	10:33	14
Beaumont	08:00	10:38	10
Cumberland Infirmary		10:50	
West Tower Street	08:13	10:56	10
Carlisle Bus Station	08:18	11:01	12

93 Service

Bus Stop	Time	Time	Time	Time	See page
Carlisle Bus Station	12:50	16:30	18:10	†	12
West Tower Street	12:54	16:34	18:14	19:37	12
Cumberland Infirmary	13:00				
Beaumont	13:11	16:48	18:28	19:24	16
Burgh by Sands	13:16	16:53	18:33	19:19	18
Dykesfield	13:19	16:56	18:36	19:16	22
Drumburgh	13:24	17:01	18:41	19:11	24
Glasson	13:28	17:05	18:45	19:07	26
Port Carlisle	13:33	17:10	18:50	19:02	28
Bowness on Solway	13:37	17:14	↳18:55 ↱		28
Cardurnock	13:49				34
Anthorn	13:55	17:28	The last bus of the day turns around at Bowness and retraces its route back to Carlisle		38
Kirkbride	14:06	17:38			42
Kirkbampton	14:16	17:48			44
Thurstonfield	14:18	17:50			44
Moorhouse	14:21	17:53			44
West Tower Street	14:33	18:05			44
Carlisle Bus Station	14:36	18:08			44

† The last bus of the day does not call at the Bus Station.

Carlisle

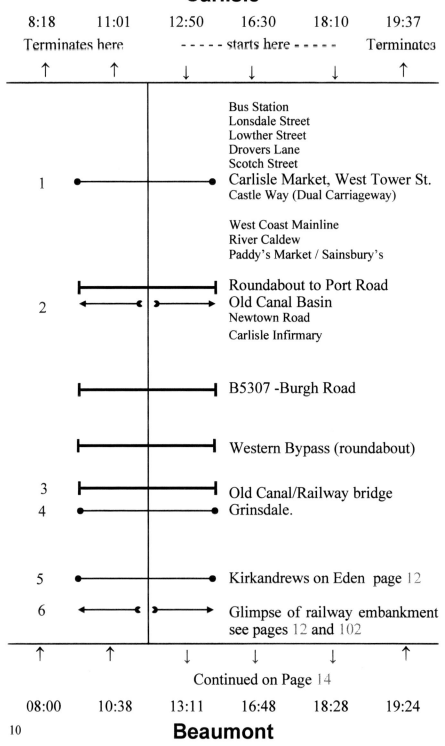

| 8:18 | 11:01 | 12:50 | 16:30 | 18:10 | 19:37 |

Terminates here   - - - - - starts here - - - - -   Terminates

↑   ↑   ↓   ↓   ↓   ↑

Bus Station
Lonsdale Street
Lowther Street
Drovers Lane
Scotch Street

1   Carlisle Market, West Tower St.
Castle Way (Dual Carriageway)

West Coast Mainline
River Caldew
Paddy's Market / Sainsbury's

2   Roundabout to Port Road
Old Canal Basin
Newtown Road
Carlisle Infirmary

B5307 -Burgh Road

Western Bypass (roundabout)

3   Old Canal/Railway bridge
4   Grinsdale.

5   Kirkandrews on Eden page 12

6   Glimpse of railway embankment
see pages 12 and 102

↑   ↑   ↓   ↓   ↓   ↑

Continued on Page 14

| 08:00 | 10:38 | 13:11 | 16:48 | 18:28 | 19:24 |

Beaumont

1. **The Market Hall.** Carlisle boasts one of few remaining covered Victorian markets. Built by Arthur Cawston and Joseph Graham of Westminster for the Carlisle Corporation between 1887 and 1889, using ironwork manufactured by Cowans, Sheldon and Company, who were a local company based down the London Road in Carlisle. The market is open Monday to Saturday from 8am to 5pm but the individual stalls, selling a variety of goods including fresh fish, meat, vegetables, haberdashery and stationery may have different opening times. Also located within the Market Hall are cafes and toilets as well as two national retail outlets. There are several bus stops outside the Market and are shown on the timetable as being West Tower Street.

2. The canal that linked the city with its port started near the Jovial Sailor pub in what is now the Port Road Business Park. Nothing remains of the canal today. Opposite the Jovial Sailor is a children's playground and close to the pub is the remains of a railway bridge that used to take trains over the road from the Citadel Station to Port Carlisle. After the Canal Company was forced to close, it was drained and the railway laid in its channel - see page 102.

3. We cross over the old canal/railway at a bridge on an S-bend near Grinsdale.

4. There is a request stop for Grinsdale close to the old canal/railway bridge. Grinsdale itself is about ¾ mile (1 km) down a lane off the main road. Hadrian's Wall Path can be accessed at Grinsdale, (Walk 1 page 48), and also Grinsdale Church, (Walk 2 on page 49).

5. The kirk (church) of St. Andrews, was demolished a long time ago and its place is marked only by its graveyard, where St.Andrew's well can be found. The bus does not pass the former Kirkandrews Railway station, which is now a private dwelling. However it is but a short walk from the bus stop along the main road. Passengers should alight here for Hollow Creek Self Catering Holiday Cottage.

6. Between Kirkandrews and Beaumont you can just glimpse the artificially flat embankment of the old railway see page 102

Kirkandrews

This is a request stop so does not show on the timetable, but they are a few points of interest. The short walks described here start at the Bus Stop.

The Old Railway Station						
Miles	Metres	OS Map	GPS	↓	↑	Remarks
		353 584	54.916325, -3.009759			From the bus stop walk along the short road to the main Carlisle-Bowness Road
				Turn Right	Turn Left	
0.13	200	352 585	54.916379, -3.012356			
The old Station is now a private dwelling. The road used to be carried over the railway on a bridge but this was damaged in the 1970's and has since been removed						

The Old Churchyard						
Miles	Metres	OS Map	GPS	↓	↑	Remarks
		353 584	54.916325, -3.009759			From the bus stop walk along road towards Beaumont.
0.01	17	353 586	54.916771, -3.010012			

Hadrian's Wall Path						
Miles	Metres	OS Map	GPS	↓	↑	Remarks
		353 584	54.916325, -3.009759			From the bus stop walk along the short road to the main Carlisle-Bowness Road towards Carlisle, which is the route the bus takes.
0.1	155	354 583	54.915284, -3.008152	Turn left	Turn Right	Public footpath is marked
0.06	100	355 584	54.916079, -3.007547			Hadrian's Wall Path is described in Walk 1
				Turn left	Turn Right	For Beaumont
				Turn Right	Turn left	For Grinsdale
0.05	86	355 583	54.914874, -3.007017			Instead of turning onto the public footpath, carry on the main road for the Hollow Creek Self Catering Cottage

Beaumont

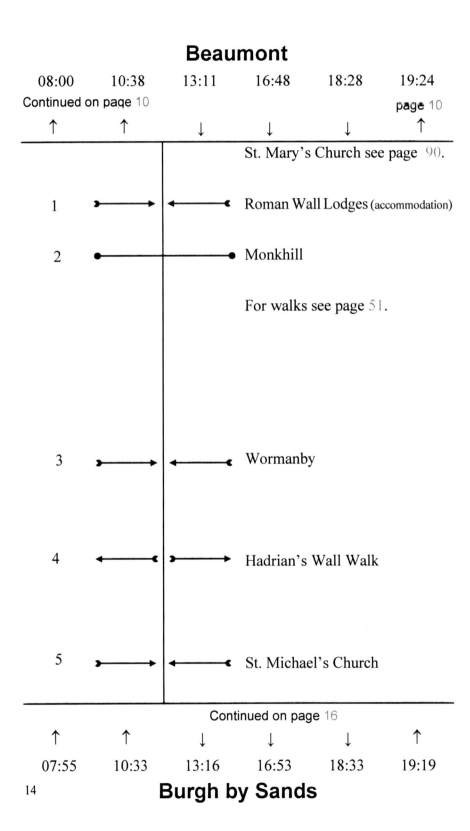

08:00   10:38   13:11   16:48   18:28   19:24

Continued on page 10   page 10

↑   ↑   ↓   ↓   ↓   ↑

St. Mary's Church see page 90.

1   Roman Wall Lodges (accommodation)

2   Monkhill

For walks see page 51.

3   Wormanby

4   Hadrian's Wall Walk

5   St. Michael's Church

Continued on page 16

↑   ↑   ↓   ↓   ↓   ↑

07:55   10:33   13:16   16:53   18:33   19:19

Burgh by Sands

Pronounced Bee-mont, the name is a translation from the French meaning 'beautiful mount'. The Solway was fordable near here and used by drovers to bring their cattle from Scotland into England. The Drovers Rest Pub in nearby Monkhill is testimony to this traffic of old.

1. The road crosses over the old canal/railway. Although the bridge has since been demolished. Its location is marked by Lock House (now a private dwelling). On the opposite side of the road are the Roman Wall Lodges providing a variety of accommodation facilities. For further information telephone Martin Doherty Telephone 07784 736423 or browse http://www.hadrians-wall-accommodation.co.uk/

2. The request bus stop is located at the cross-roads on the Monkhill-Beaumont road outside the Methodist Chapel. At this cross roads the bus continues on the main Carlisle to Burgh road. Walkers following this road back towards Carlisle will find themselves outside the Drovers Rest after walking only a few yards. The public house is open between 12:00 and 23:00 providing food, drink and toilet facilities. For more information about when food is served, telephone 01228 576141.

   The fourth road at the cross roads provides a 1½ miles (2.4km) walk to Moorhouse, where the 93 Bus can be rejoined, but there is little of interest along the route and a fairly long wait to catch the bus at the other end.

3. The old canal/railway bridge at Wormanby has been demolished in recent years due to road improvements. The Bus will stop near here on request for passengers to alight on Walk 5 to Moorhouse (see page 53, but if walking the opposite way, from Moorhouse to Wormanby, it is better to walk a few extra yards to catch the bus at Burgh - or better still while away the time in the Greyhound Inn in Burgh.

4. Hadrian's Walk Trail can be accessed here - see page 52.

5. St Michael's Church can be seen on approaching Burgh by Sands and a description is given on page 16.

Burgh by Sands

Continued on page 14   page 14

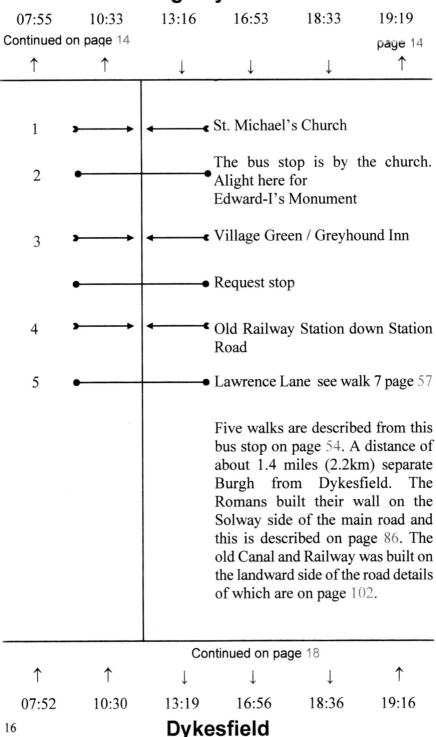

1 St. Michael's Church

2 The bus stop is by the church. Alight here for Edward-I's Monument

3 Village Green / Greyhound Inn

   Request stop

4 Old Railway Station down Station Road

5 Lawrence Lane see walk 7 page 57

Five walks are described from this bus stop on page 54. A distance of about 1.4 miles (2.2km) separate Burgh from Dykesfield. The Romans built their wall on the Solway side of the main road and this is described on page 86. The old Canal and Railway was built on the landward side of the road details of which are on page 102.

Continued on page 18

07:52   10:30   13:19   16:56   18:36   19:16

Dykesfield

The English language can be quite illogical at times and the spelling of Burgh is just one of those occasions since it is pronounced 'bruff'. In Roman times it was known as Aballava, so they had no problems with the pronunciation!

1. St. Michael's Church dates from the 12th century but restored in 1881. The stones used in its construction were taken from Hadrian's Wall or from Aballava fort. Most of the older buildings on the Bowness Peninsular used this method of recycling, which is why nothing can be seen of the original wall in the area from here to Brampton. It was in this church that King Edward- I's body was laid out after his death on the nearby marsh. The Church is described on page 92.

2. Edward-I, known as 'The Hammer of the Scots' died a short walk away from here on 7th July 1307 during a campaign against the Scottish king, Robert the Bruce. The Latin inscription on Edward's monument translates as "The Greatest English King". It was he who initiated the Hundred Years War with France and three hundred years of fighting with Scotland. He instructed his son to avenge his death, but Robert the Bruce was able to capture large parts of what is now Cumbria. Walk 6 on page 56 passes King Edward's Monument. Why the king should be here in the first place is described on page 97 and his royal ancestry is charted on page 21.

3. The Village Green and Wildlife Area was opened in 2010 primarily as a home for the village cricket team and as a community resource provided by the Burgh by Sands Sports and Recreation Association. The monument standing guard over the area is of King Edward-1. The location of the old railway track can be visualised by the artificially flat ground at the far end of the Green. The Greyhound Inn, is open seven days a week from noon. Food is served between noon and 2pm (3pm at the weekend) and from 5:30 to 8pm (except Monday evenings) Telephone 01228 576579 for further details or browse http://www.thegreyhoundinn-burgh.co.uk/

4. The Old Railway station in Burgh is now a private residence that can be reached down Station Road.

5. Go Cumbria Motorhome Hire is conveniently placed near this request stop for anyone preferring to explore further afield than the bus route. It is such a popular service that they are often booked up months in advance, so best to telephone them on 07547 727266, although email is prefered from their website: http://gocumbriamotorhomehire.co.uk/

Dykesfield

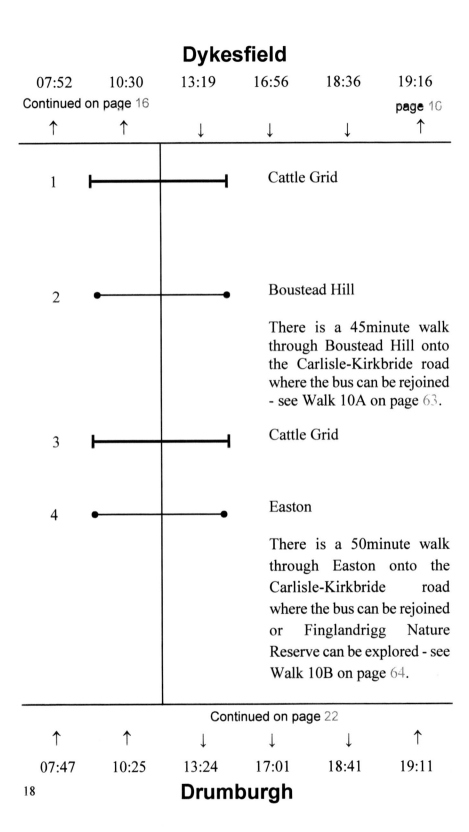

07:52   10:30   13:19   16:56   18:36   19:16

Continued on page 16   page 16

↑   ↑   ↓   ↓   ↓   ↑

1   Cattle Grid

2   Boustead Hill

There is a 45minute walk through Boustead Hill onto the Carlisle-Kirkbride road where the bus can be rejoined - see Walk 10A on page 63.

3   Cattle Grid

4   Easton

There is a 50minute walk through Easton onto the Carlisle-Kirkbride road where the bus can be rejoined or Finglandrigg Nature Reserve can be explored - see Walk 10B on page 64.

Continued on page 22

↑   ↑   ↓   ↓   ↓   ↑

07:47   10:25   13:24   17:01   18:41   19:11

Drumburgh

The Cattle Grid at Dykesfield

The road junction at Dykesfield leads to Longburgh village just a few hundred yards down the road. The road provides a quiet country lane walk linking to Thurstonfield some 1¾ miles (2.9km) away from where the 93 bus can be rejoined. *En route* why not relax in Longburgh Pool where an hour session can be booked in a swimming pool Digitally controlled for a constant temperature of 32°C, Longburgh Pool is probably the warmest pool in Cumbria which makes it a very pleasant experience for everyone. It is especially suitable for young children, pensioners, those convalescing after illness and non swimmers. For more information browse http://longburghpool.co.uk/ or telephone 01228 576435.

1. The cattle grid at Dykesfield marks the eastern end of Burgh Marsh. The raised embankment protected the railway from tidal flooding and today provides an ideal footpath. Along the road are posts advising the depth of water at high tide. Care should be taken in walking on the marsh itself because when the tide is incoming the water level rises so quickly that a person is unable to out-run it - see Beware the Tides of March on page 117. When, in the 1970's, the author moved into the area, there was a tower on Burgh Marsh. It was a substantial staircase leading to an enclosed platform where people cut off by the tide could sit out the danger. It fell into disrepair and since nobody has ever used it as a means of escaping the dangerous tide it was decided to demolish it. Paradoxically, one week before demolition began a couple were in danger from an abnormally high tide and were the first people to seek the refuge of the tower.

Boustead Hill

2. The large prominent houses at Boustead Hill is where some of the directors of the canal company lived. From the vantage point of the drumlin they could overlook their investment. Today it is a farming village and also the location of the Boustead Hill Equestrian Centre The Beeches Farm. It is a friendly up and coming establishment, owned and run by Sarah Reay who offers horse riding lessons in Cumbria with excellent tuition and an enjoyable time. For more information telephone 01228 575000 or browse http://www.bousteadhillec.co.uk/

Highfield Farm Bed & Breakfast is a unique and special place to stay at Boustead Hill. They offer 'walk & stay' and 'Walk & Pitch' overlooking the Solway Firth. Martin and Julie offer a warm Cumbrian welcome to their guests, all of whom enjoy the breathtaking landscape, the hospitality and that very special feeling that comes with a truly relaxing home. They are a short walk from the bus stop - see page 63. For more information telephone 01228 576060 or browse http://highfield-holidays.co.uk

3. The cattle grid splits the marsh in half and marks the parish boundary between Burgh and Bowness and also between Allerdale and Carlisle Borough Councils.

4. Easton is a small farming community in the centre of which is Midtown Farm where Janice Byers fills her kitchen with the smell of freshly baked bread. Guests in her B&B are also treated to her homemade granola breakfast pots, cookies, marmalade and jam. Her packed lunches contain home baked flapjacks and she buys in locally produced bacon, eggs, sausage, and dairy products. To sample these treats yourself telephone Janice on 01228 576550 or browse her website: http://midtown-farm.co.uk/

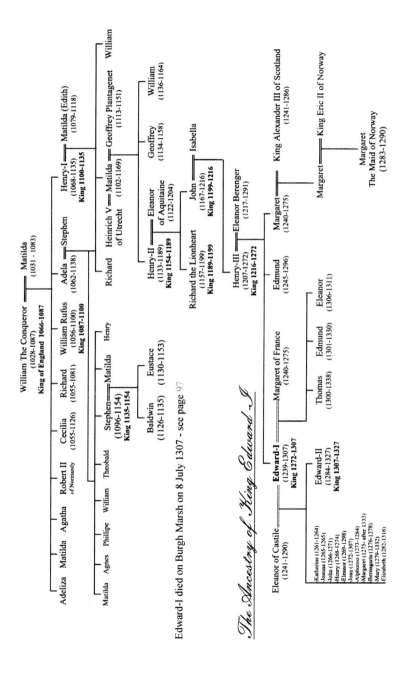

William The Conqueror
(1028-1087)
King of England 1066-1087
═══ Matilda
(1031 - 1083)

Adeliza | Matilda | Agatha | Robert II | Cecilia | Richard | William Rufus | Adela | Henry-I | Matilda (Edith) | William
 | | | of Normandy | (1055-1126) | (1055-1081) | (1056-1100) | (1062-1138) | (1068-1135) | (1079-1118) |
 | | | | | | **King 1087-1100** | ═ Stephen | **King 1100-1135** |

Matilda | Agnes | Phillipe | William | Theobald | Stephen ═══ Matilda | Henry | Richard | Heinrich V ═══ Matilda ═══ Geoffrey Plantagenet
 | | | | | (1096-1154) | | | of Utrecht | (1102-1169) | (1113-1151)
 | | | | | **King 1135-1154** | | | | |

Baldwin | Eustace
(1126-1135) | (1130-1153)

Geoffrey | William
(1134-1158) | (1136-1164)

Henry-II ═══ Eleanor
(1133-1189) | of Aquitaine
King 1154-1189 | (1122-1204)

Richard the Lionheart | John ═══ Isabella
(1157-1199) | (1167-1216) | (1217-1291)
King 1189-1199 | **King 1199-1216**

Henry-III ═══ Eleanor Berenger
(1207-1272)
King 1216-1272

Edmund | Margaret ═══ King Alexander III of Scotland
(1245-1296) | (1240-1275) | (1241-1286)

Margaret ═══ King Eric II of Norway

Margaret
The Maid of Norway
(1283-1290)

Edward-I died on Burgh Marsh on 8 July 1307 - see page 97

The Ancestry of King Edward-I

Eleanor of Castile ═══ **Edward-I** ═══ Margaret of France
(1241-1290) | (1239-1307) | (1240-1275)
 | **King 1272-1307** |

Edward-II | Thomas | Edmund | Eleanor
(1284-1327) | (1300-1338) | (1301-1330) | (1306-1311)
King 1307-1327 | | |

Katherine (1261-1264)
Joanna (1265-1265)
John (1266-1271)
Henry (1268-1274)
Eleanor (1269-1298)
Joan (1272-1307)
Alphonso (1273-1284)
Margaret (1275- after 1333)
Berengaria (1276-1278)
Mary (1279-1332)
Elizabeth (1282-1316)

Drumburgh

| 07:47 | 10:25 | 13:24 | 17:01 | 18:41 | 19:11 |

Continued on page 18 page 10

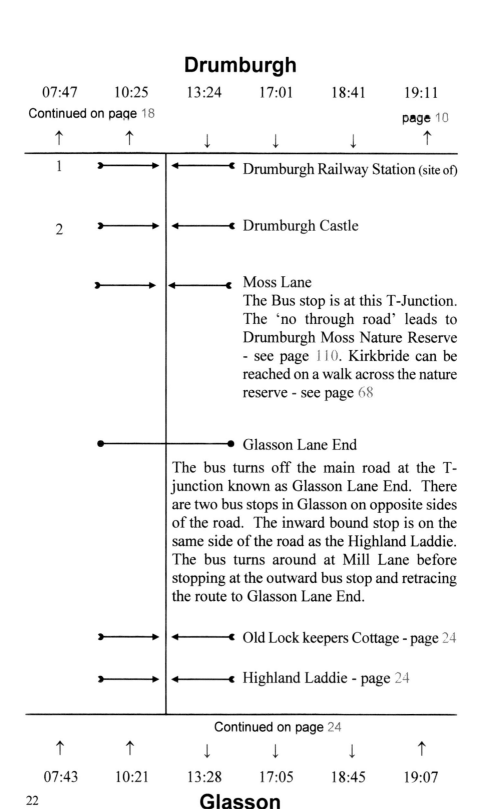

1   Drumburgh Railway Station (site of)

2   Drumburgh Castle

Moss Lane
The Bus stop is at this T-Junction. The 'no through road' leads to Drumburgh Moss Nature Reserve - see page 110. Kirkbride can be reached on a walk across the nature reserve - see page 68

Glasson Lane End

The bus turns off the main road at the T-junction known as Glasson Lane End. There are two bus stops in Glasson on opposite sides of the road. The inward bound stop is on the same side of the road as the Highland Laddie. The bus turns around at Mill Lane before stopping at the outward bus stop and retracing the route to Glasson Lane End.

Old Lock keepers Cottage - page 24

Highland Laddie - page 24

Continued on page 24

| 07:43 | 10:21 | 13:28 | 17:05 | 18:45 | 19:07 |

Glasson

In the old Celtic language 'Drum' means 'ridge near the fort' and Burgh refers to Burgh-by-Sands - thus 'Drumburgh' means 'ridge near the fort at Burgh' In 1539 the Reverand John Leland visited the area and commented that Hadrian's Wall had been robbed of its stone in order to construct Drumburgh Castle.

1. Just before approaching Drumburgh from the Carlisle Direction an area of flattened land that carried the canal and railway, sweeps toward the Solway. A tarmac path leading to a park bench was the original main road in the time of the railway and before the road was straightened and improved into today's highway. Almost level with the park bench and on the opposite side of the road is a private dwelling that used to be Drumburgh Railway Station. From the station the Carlisle line splits. One branch going to Port Carlisle (the sweep of flat land towards the Solway). The Kirkbride-Silloth branch is difficult to spot from the bus. It carried holiday makers from Carlisle for a day out at the seaside resort of Silloth. In 1856 passengers changed at Drumburgh for Port Carlisle and were carried there by a horse-drawn railway carriage called *The Dandy,* now on display in the York Railway Museum. Pictures of *The Dandy* are shown within the chapter on The Port Carlisle Line on page 102.

2. Drumburgh Castle is now a private dwelling that was fully restored in the 1970's. It was built in the 14th century by Thomas, Lord Dacre, who placed his coat of arms over the entrance at second floor level. The older Pele tower was crenellated in 1307 under a licence granted to Robert le Brun. Jacob Harington inherited it through marriage in the 15th century but let the castle fall into disrepair. There is a date-stone over the upper doorway which testifies that it was restored in 1518. The castle provided a safe refuge against attacks from the Border Reivers.

Drumburgh Castle

Glasson

07:43   10:21   13:28   17:05   18:45   19:07

Continued on page 22   page 22

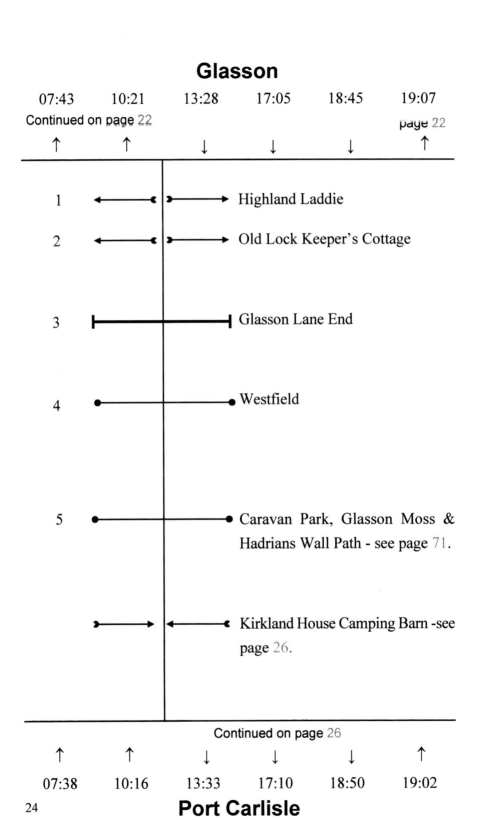

1   Highland Laddie

2   Old Lock Keeper's Cottage

3   Glasson Lane End

4   Westfield

5   Caravan Park, Glasson Moss & Hadrians Wall Path - see page 71.

Kirkland House Camping Barn -see page 26.

Continued on page 26

07:38   10:16   13:33   17:10   18:50   19:02

Port Carlisle

Like everywhere in this area nothing remains of the Roman Wall in Glasson, but in the 18th century a sandstone building stone was found near Glasson inscribed "Legions II Aug Coh III". The Hadrian's Wall Path passes along the main road in the village - see page 71.

1. The Highland Laddie provides accommodation, food and drink. The landlord is an experienced Haaf-Net Fisherman and uses the fresh fish he catches in the Solway in his restaurant. The service he provides also involves taking clients into the Solway Estuary with giant nets and potentially catching fish. At the end of the day his experienced chefs will prepare and cook the visitor's catch. The Highland Laddie also serves local beer in its well-stocked bar. For more information browse http://haafnettersfishing.co.uk/ or telephone 016973 51839.

2. The old railway/canal passed under a bridge located between the Highland Laddie and the main road. Here stands a private dwelling called "The Old Lockkeeper's Cottage". (It is the cottage that is old not the lock keeper). The single platform station was located here. It had a small shelter. The bridge was originally a drawbridge but was later increased in height to convert it to a railway bridge.

3. The bus leaves/re-joins the main road at a T-junction known as Glasson Lane End.

4. Westfield is a small hamlet on an embankment overlooking the Solway. This stretch of the Solway is the favourite place for the Haaf-Net Fishermen.

5. The bus will stop on request at a T-Junction which gives access to the Cottage and Glendale Holiday Park. A restaurant serves the residents and walkers. For more information browse http://www.cottageandglendale.com or telephone 016973 51317.

Just to the Port Carlisle side of this junction is the site of Roman Milecastle 78 - see page 89. Further down the lane is the Glasson Moss National Nature Reserve, further information is given on page 111. On the opposite side of the main road, Hadrian's Wall Path continues along what used to be the old railway (and canal) - see page 102.

Port Carlisle

07:38	10:16	13:33	17:10	18:50	19:02

Continued on page 24 page 24

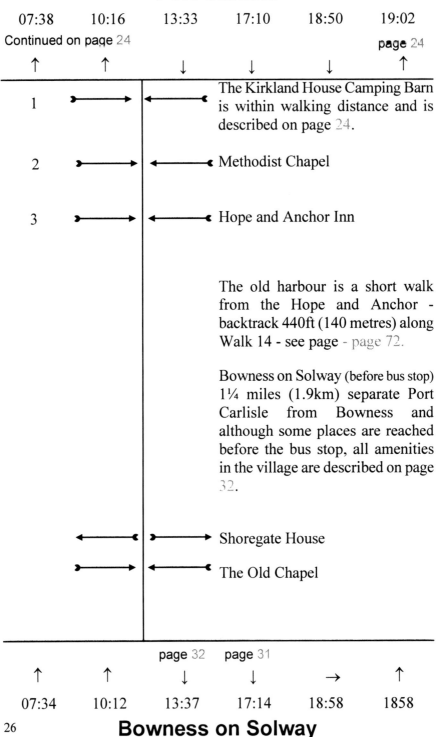

1 The Kirkland House Camping Barn is within walking distance and is described on page 24.

2 Methodist Chapel

3 Hope and Anchor Inn

The old harbour is a short walk from the Hope and Anchor - backtrack 440ft (140 metres) along Walk 14 - see page - page 72.

Bowness on Solway (before bus stop) 1¼ miles (1.9km) separate Port Carlisle from Bowness and although some places are reached before the bus stop, all amenities in the village are described on page 32.

Shoregate House

The Old Chapel

page 32   page 31

07:34	10:12	13:37	17:14	18:58	1858

Bowness on Solway

Carlisle's port at Sandsfield was no longer suitable for shipping and alternative sites were considered. Finally Fisher's Cross was chosen and a canal from Caldewgate, Carlisle to Fisher's Cross was completed in 1823 whereupon Fisher's Cross was renamed Port Carlisle. Seagoing vessels of up to 100 tons could use the canal to reach Carlisle. The canal closed on 1 August 1853 to be replaced by the railway, which was completed fifteen months later - see page 101 for a more detailed history. The station was located on what is now the Bowling Club car park. The picture below, taken in the early part of the 20th century, shows the Bowling Club existed at the same time as the station.

1. Chapel Side Camping and Caravanning Site & Kirkland House Camping Barn provides overnight accommodation Telephone Daphne Hogg on 016973 51400 for further information.

2. The Methodist Chapel was built in 1861. It has a kitchen where tourists are invited to serve themselves with tea or coffee or to use the microwave. Toilet facilities are also available.

3. The Hope and Anchor is now run by Rebecca Edgar, who as well as providing the hospitality of a village pub, also has a tea room where she serves freshly baked scones, cakes and homemade soups. Ask her for her speciality - lumpy bumpy hot chocolate - wow! The Hope and Anchor is usually open between noon and 11pm for more information telephone Beccy on 016973 51460.

Between Port Carlisle and Bowness excellent views of the Solway can be seen. Look out for the tidal bore, which is no less impressive than the Bristol Channel's famous Severn Bore. Both caused by the tide being funnelled into the estuary and forming a distinctive step moving up the estuary. The times of the tide can be found by referring to page 117.

Bowness on Solway

07:34   10:12   13:37   17:14   18:58   1858

↑   ↑   ↓   ↓   ↓   ↑

The bus service has three routes when it gets to Bowness. All routes pass the Kings Arms. One route, outlined on page 32, travels past the Lindow Hall, the Church and a hamlet called Millrigg and on towards Anthorn. The more interesting route is via Cardurnock and this is described on page 33. The last bus of the day terminates in Bowness and turns around just past the School then retraces its path back to Carlisle Market (it does not go to the Bus Station).

Bus stop   Lindow Hall

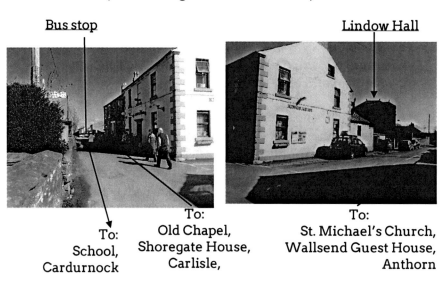

To:
Old Chapel,
To: Shoregate House,
School,   Carlisle,
Cardurnock

To:
St. Michael's Church,
Wallsend Guest House,
Anthorn

The western end of Hadrian's Wall terminated in the Roman fort called 'Maia'. In Greek mythology Maia was one of the seven sisters or Pleiades, but the Romans associated her with growth and the adjective 'larger'. The fort here was larger than Segedunum - the equivalent fort at the eastern end of the Wall.

Nothing obvious remains of Maia today, its stones being re-used in the construction of houses and barns in the area. The Roman Granary is thought to have been on the site now occupied by the church dedicated to St. Michael. The church was built in the 12th century and restored in the 18th. In 1626 the church bells were stolen in a raid by the border reivers. Unfortunately, the boat that they used was unable to carry the weight of the bells and in order to save their lives the bells were jettisoned. They now lie at the bottom of the Solway in what is know known as the

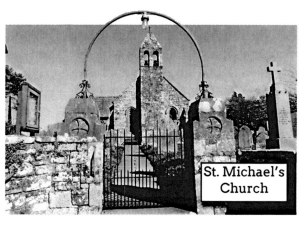

St. Michael's Church

Bell Pool. If you stand near the shore at Bowness on a stormy night it is said that you can still hear the bells ringing. Unable to summon the faithful to church, the locals then stole the bells from Middlebie church in Dumfriesshire. For many years when a new rector was installed in Bowness, he received a request from his Scottish counterpart asking for their bells back, to which he replied, "certainly, when you return ours." Similar correspondence ceased in more recent years.

Years ago public houses in Scotland were closed on Sundays, unlike the English ones. Taking advantage of the Solway Viaduct, which the Caledonian Railway constructed to carry its line between Annan and Bowness, the Scots walked to the King's Arms in Bowness, (see page 33). Today the King's Arms serves food as well as drink. For further information telephone 016973 51426 or browse http://www.kingsarmsbowness.co.uk.

The Lindow Hall was donated by Samuel Lindow, who was a major landowner at the end of the 19th century. He was born at Wood End, Egremont about 1850 the son of John and Eleanor Lindow. In 1911 he was rector of Bowness-on-Solway. The hall serves as the village hall and community centre and often stages theatrical performances. The Lindow Hall provides overnight accommodation for visitors to Bowness-on-Solway at the start/end of Hadrian's Wall. Both small and large groups can sleep in the bunk beds upstairs. Other facilities include a large kitchen and eating area, separate male/female hot showers and toilets. Secure bicycle storage and additional sleeper space is provided in the main hall area. To book the Bunk Room telephone Marcia Leonard on 016973 52487 or browse their website at http://www.lindowhall.org.uk

Past the Lindow Hall and the Church is the Old Rectory which is now Wallsend Guest House. They offer quality 4-star bed and breakfast accommodation and are proud to have received a gold award from Enjoy England in recognition of the quality of their rooms, breakfast and overall customer service. Their tea-room is open between Easter and the end of September. They also have luxury 'Wigwam' cabins that sleep four with *en suite* facilities for those wanting a self-catering holiday. A tent campsite is also available. For more information telephone 016973 51055 or browse http://www.wallsend.net/.

There is more accommodation in Bowness along the Carlisle Road. A short walk from the King's Arms is the Old Chapel. Maureen and Michael Miller bought the chapel and cottage to save it from being demolished a number of years ago. There has been a great deal of structural and renovation work undertaken by local tradesmen, resulting in a sympathetic conversion of the building, to provide ideal accommodation for the many visitors to our area. Their own home is situated next door to the chapel, therefore guests have the freedom of using the accommodation provisions but will know they are on hand should they be needed. For further information telephone 016973 51126. Alternatively, visit their website http://www.oldchapelbownessonsolway.com.

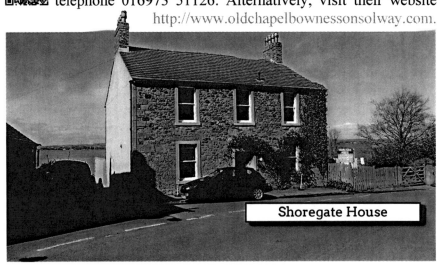

Shoregate House

Shoregate House was once a corn mill that dates back to 1684 and today provides Bed and Breakfast. For more information telephone Alan Graham on 016973 51308 or browse http://www.shoregatehouse.co.uk/

Bowness on Solway

07:34   17:14

Continued on page 26

↑   ↓

In order to avoid duplication, the items of interest on this route are described elsewhere.	described on page 28.	Kings Arms Lindow Hall St. Michael's Church Wallsend Guest House
		Millrigg Glasson Lane End
		Whitrigg Triangle
		Whitrigg
	described on page 38.	Rogersceugh Longcroft
		Anthorn
		Anthorn Radio Station

page 34

↑   ↓

07:20   17:28

Anthorn

Bowness on Solway

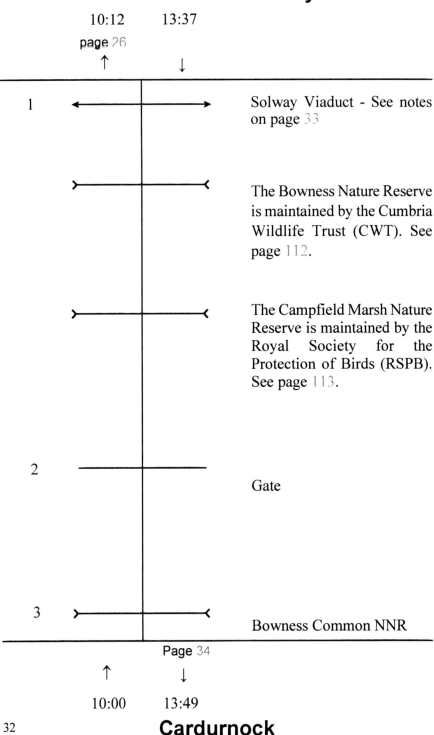

10:12   13:37

page 26

↑   ↓

1   Solway Viaduct - See notes on page 33

The Bowness Nature Reserve is maintained by the Cumbria Wildlife Trust (CWT). See page 112.

The Campfield Marsh Nature Reserve is maintained by the Royal Society for the Protection of Birds (RSPB). See page 113.

2   Gate

3   Bowness Common NNR

Page 34

↑   ↓

10:00   13:49

Cardurnock

Opposite the school *circa 1910*
Remains of the viaduct can still be seen

The bus passes three nature reserves on this part of the journey; Bowness Nature Reserve, Campfield Marsh Nature Reserve and Bowness Common National Nature Reserve (at Cardurnock).

1. Standing on the road near Bowness school at the beginning of the 20th century, the view above the rooftops of the low-lying houses, revealed trains puffing across the one-mile long Solway Viaduct linking Bowness Station with Annan. The Solway Viaduct used to carry the Caledonian Railway between Bowness and Annan to bring iron ore from West Cumberland to Scotland. Until then this traffic was routed via Carlisle, but the viaduct offered a much shorter route. - See page - page 107.

2. A gate across the road prevents cattle grazing on the marsh from straying. It is only closed at the farmer's discretion when cattle are on the marsh. Please keep the gate closed if you find it in that condition.

3. Just before the Cardurnock bus stop, but within the hamlet boundary, is a small area of common land often used for parking farm vehicles. This is Cardurnock Pond whose waters were drained many years ago. I was told this was to prevent children accidentally drowning. A footpath from here leads to Bowness Common, see page 114.

Cardurnock

page 32

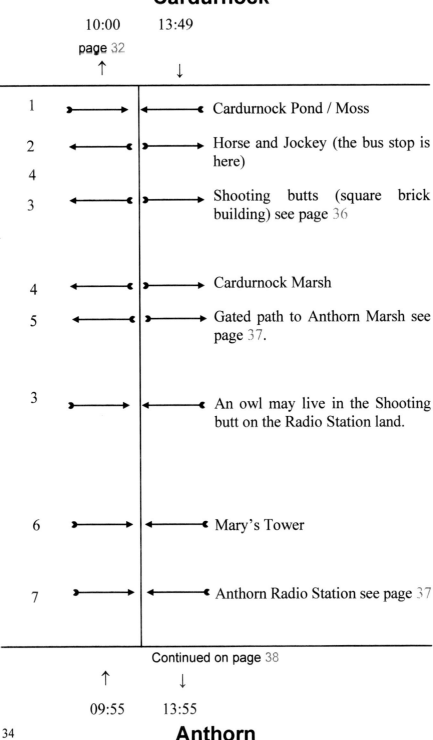

	10:00	13:49	
	↑	↓	
1	→	←	Cardurnock Pond / Moss
2 4	←	→	Horse and Jockey (the bus stop is here)
3	←	→	Shooting butts (square brick building) see page 36
4	←	→	Cardurnock Marsh
5	←	→	Gated path to Anthorn Marsh see page 37.
3	→	←	An owl may live in the Shooting butt on the Radio Station land.
6	→	←	Mary's Tower
7	→	←	Anthorn Radio Station see page 37

Continued on page 38

↑   ↓

09:55   13:55

Anthorn

In the centre of the hamlet is a footpath that leads to Cardurnock Marsh. Never use this path near high tide as the tide frequently comes on the landward side of the gate blocking a safe return - see page 117. However, at low neap tide Longdyke Scar can be seen between Cardurnock and Anthorn. Here the sand gives way to a 'pebbly place'. Cardurnock translated from the Old English means 'The Fort Near The Pebbly Place'.

The Roman fort at Cardurnock can no longer be seen but was excavated recently. The footpath leading from Cardurock to the Marsh has a second lonning (lane) joining it at a right angle just 100 metres from the main road. This second lonning ran on the landward side of the Roman Defences. The lonning comes to an end after only a few metres but the fort was in the next field and on the Solway side of the lonning. The Roman defences linked up to Hadrian's Wall at Bowness and extended south as far as Maryport.

1. Just to the north of the main part of the hamlet is the old pond, which has been filled in many years ago and now often used to park farm vehicles etc. The lonning leading from it gives access to Cardunock Moss, part of the Bowness Common National Nature Reserve - see page 114.

2. The bus stop for Cardurnock is outside the Horse and Jockey. As its name suggests this used to be a public house but has been a private dwelling for many years. The author lived here for about 25 years. It lacked a traditional bar. Drinks were brought from the cellar by the bar maid to the public rooms. On one occasion a reveler rode his horse through the front door, down the passageway and out the back, much to the amusement of the drinkers - I was not so pleased that the house we had bought had been so abused!

Horse and Jockey

Wild geese in front of old shooting butt

3. The square brick buildings, of which there are several between Cardurnock and Anthorn, were at the end of each runway when what is now a radio station was a Royal Naval airfield during the First and Second World Wars. The brick buildings were used as shooting butts to test the aircraft's guns at take-off. If you are lucky you may see an owl using the one on the radio station as a nesting site.

4. Cadurnock Marsh, and the land adjacent to it, support large flocks of birds, more details of which are on page 116. In addition it is the home of the rare natterjack toad. Ten years ago only 20-30 were spotted but more recently they have increased to over 150. I spoke to a sound recordist who was recording them and he told me he also recorded a similar group of natterjacks just over the border in Scotland. They have a slightly different accent to the Anthorn toads.

5. Solway House, a farm of 320 acres, was demolished to make way for the wartime airfield. A path linked the house with the marsh and this path with a gate to the marsh is all that is left to mark its location.

6. Mary's Tower can be seen on a small hill behind the radio station. It is a folly, now used as a farm building, and built in the 1850's for Mary Backhouse, an accomplished artist, to use as a studio. There are windows on

    Mary's Tower

    all four sides of the tower for her to capture breathtaking landscapes of the area. Mary was born in Burgh by Sands about 1827 the daughter of Robert and Dorothy Backhouse and would have been in her early twenties when the tower was built. Robert was a prosperous farmer employing four live-in servants on his 140 acre farm at Anthorn, so was obviously able to afford to build the tower for his daughter. Some researchers think the tower is associated with Mary, Queen of Scots, but this is erroneous as it was only built in 1850 and not in the 16th century. Furthermore, it is thought that Mary landed at Workington on her way to Carlisle and this route would not pass Anthorn.

7. The Anthorn Radio Station entrance is where the 93 bus turns around when bypassing Cardurnock and travelling through Millrigg, see page 31. What is now the entrance to the Radio Station used to be the way locals travelled from Anthorn to Cardurnock and vice versa using the network of runways. When in 1962 work began on building the radio station a new public highway, (the one now used by the 93 bus and all other traffic), was constructed. The tallest mast (the central one) is 900 feet high and the others 600. Originally a lift was used to carry staff up the mast for routine maintenance. In order to prevent getting a shock from the build-up of static electricity, they had to jump from the lift to the landing platform without holding on to the mast for support. Thankfully in today's era dominated by Health & Safety, a different lift system is used. Originally commissioned for military purposes, it is now used to transmit signals to synchronise domestic clocks and watches as well as world-wide VLF signals

Anthorn

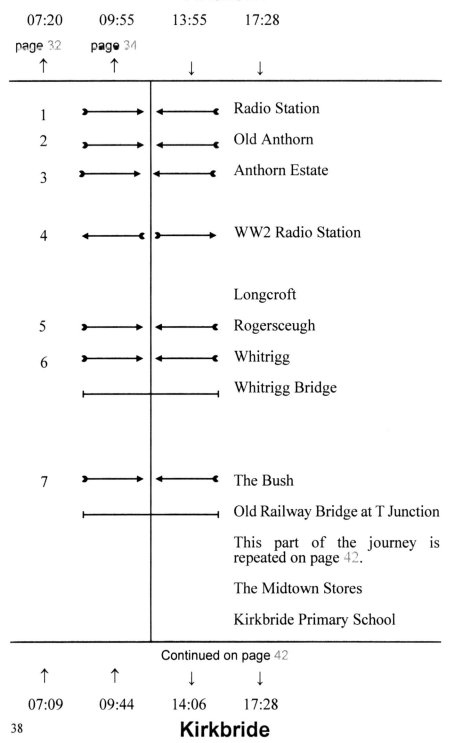

07:20	09:55	13:55	17:28	
page 32	page 34			
↑	↑	↓	↓	
1				Radio Station
2				Old Anthorn
3				Anthorn Estate
4				WW2 Radio Station
				Longcroft
5				Rogersceugh
6				Whitrigg
				Whitrigg Bridge
7				The Bush
				Old Railway Bridge at T Junction

This part of the journey is repeated on page 42.

The Midtown Stores

Kirkbride Primary School

Continued on page 42

↑	↑	↓	↓
07:09	09:44	14:06	17:28

Kirkbride

Anthorn is a translation of the Old English meaning 'the single thorn bush'. Why such a bush should be significant is unclear but it possibly marked the meeting place for Druid gatherings.

1. Depending on which bus service you are travelling on, the bus may turn round at the entrance to the Radio Station, which is discussed on page 37.

2. Anthorn is a twin village the two halves separated by about half a mile (1km). Spring tides frequently cover the road and the highest ones augmented by gale-force winds lap the gateways of the houses here - see page 117.

3. Anthorn Estate was built to house Navy Personnel during the Second World War and in the 1970's was sold off to the public.

4. Between Anthorn and Longcroft is the remains of the old Radio station used during the Second World War to communicate with aircraft.

WW2 radio station

5. Rogersceugh, a farm built on an ice-age drumlin can be seen for miles around. Now a Nature Reserve managed by the RSPB, There are many walks linking this with other nature reserves see page 113.

6. The large house on the brow of a hill is the site of the old Caledonian railway station, but the present building, built recently, is far larger than the original. See page 107 for more about the railway.

Accommodation in Anthorn

Sonya's Cottage is located in Old Anthorn (see page 38). This self-contained stables conversion is beautifully furnished throughout; with sandstone flagged floors and open vaulted ceilings revealing the original roof timbers. It offers a tranquil place to relax and enjoy the stunning views across  Moricambe Bay towards the Lake District hills. For more information telephone 016973 51771 or browse their website http://www.sonyascottage.co.uk.

Sonya's Cottage

Accommodation in Kirkbride

Three rooms are available for Bed and Breakfast in the Bush Inn. A cosy traditional country pub where Maggie offers freshly-prepared traditional home-cooked fayre. The CAMRA-approved bar is fully stocked and includes real ales. For more information telephone 01228 231496. The bus will stop by request outside the pub and this is a good base to explore the Kirkbride area - see page 81

Bush Inn

Midtown Stores

For readers walking around Kirkbride, I suggest a visit to the Midtown Stores. As well as being the local post office, it is a favourite spot for motorists and lorry drivers to buy freshly made sandwiches, snacks and drinks and for the locals to buy their groceries.

The Owl and the Wiseman at Kirkbride

Kirkbride

07:09   09:44   14:06   17:28

Continued on page 38

↑   ↑   ↓   ↓

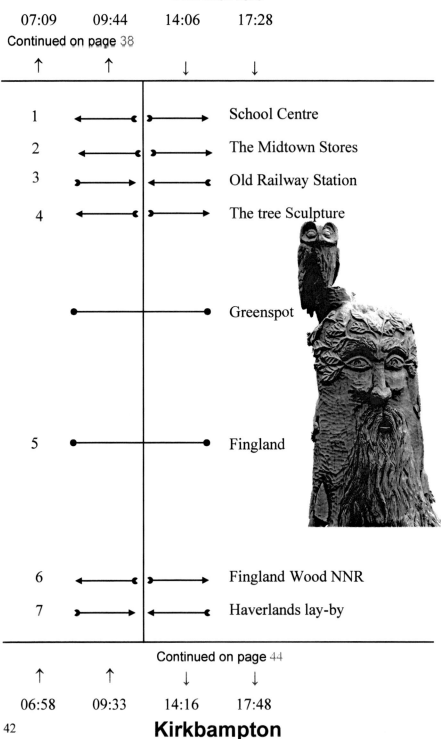

1	School Centre
2	The Midtown Stores
3	Old Railway Station
4	The tree Sculpture
	Greenspot
5	Fingland
6	Fingland Wood NNR
7	Haverlands lay-by

Continued on page 44

↑   ↑   ↓   ↓

06:58   09:33   14:16   17:48

Kirkbampton

The Church (or kirk) of St Bride gave its name to this village. Bridget, or St. Bride, was the Abbess of Kildare in sixth century Ireland. Her mother was sold as a slave to a wizard and Bridget was born in his household. One of her miracles was the conversion of the wizard and his household to Christianity.

Kirkbride Church can not be seen from the bus as it is now surrounded by tall trees on a small hill to the north of the Bush Inn. It stands on the site of the Roman fort that was built around AD80-120.

1. The bus turns around near the Primary School and retraces its route back through the village. The Kirkbride Community Centre is located at the school. For more information about the Community Centre browse http://www.kirkbridecommunity.co.uk.

2. The Midtown Stores are now the only shop/post office on the bus route. They are open Monday-Friday. For more information telephone: 016973 51231. The house adjoining the store is a listed building built probably in the late 17th century.

3. Next to the children's playground is the old school which stands in front of the old railway station, which is now a private dwelling. The railway line used to go under the bridge that carries the Kirkbride-Whitrigg road.

4. When a tree became dangerous and had to be felled, the owner, Dr John Noblett, preserved as much of the trunk as possible and carved this sculpture. The tawny owls used to live in the tree but have now migrated to nearby trees. The spirit of the tree is represented by the face with other scenes of nature carved in the trunk. Dr Noblett made the sculpture as a source of interest for children and as a means by which the tree lives on.

5. Fingland dates back to the middle ages when it was known as Thingland. Roughly translated it means 'a place of assembly'.

6. Finglandrigg Wood is a lovely wheelchair-friendly National Nature Reserve - see page 115.

7. At Haverlands House the road is very straight. Look carefully at the lay-by and you can see that this used to be a winding road.

Kirkbampton

06:58   09:33   14:16   17:48

Continued on page 42

↑   ↑   ↓   ↓

06:55   09:30   14:18   17:50

Thurstonfield

↑   ↑   ↓   ↓

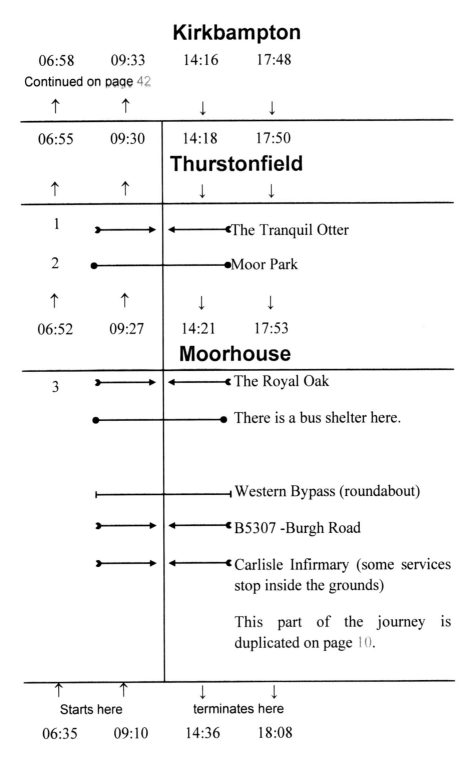

1   The Tranquil Otter

2   Moor Park

↑   ↑   ↓   ↓

06:52   09:27   14:21   17:53

Moorhouse

3   The Royal Oak

There is a bus shelter here.

Western Bypass (roundabout)

B5307 -Burgh Road

Carlisle Infirmary (some services stop inside the grounds)

This part of the journey is duplicated on page 10.

↑   ↑   ↓   ↓

Starts here   terminates here

06:35   09:10   14:36   18:08

Carlisle

There are fewer points of interest between Kirkbampton and Carlisle. However, the bus serves a large community so the stops are timetabled and described on the opposite page..

St. Peter's Church in Kirkbampton dates from Norman times and there is a Methodist Chapel in Thurstonfield- see page 96.

The Watchtree Nature Reserve is three mile walk down the road that runs past Kirkbampton School.

The name 'Thurstonfield' is probably of Viking origin as associated with Thor, their god of thunder and roughly translated means 'the field of Thor's rock'

1. The Tranquil Otter on Thurstonfield Lough is a wonderful holiday destination with its timber lodges set in a site of special scientific interest (SSSI) where you can see a variety of birds that are regularly monitored by the RSPB. For more information telephone 01228 576661, or better still, browse their excellent website at https://www.thetranquilotter.co.uk/

2. Next door to Moor Park Farm is an attractive Bed & Breakfast guest house whilst opposite Moor Park Farm is Bramble Beck Caravan Park. A family owned and run caravan park set in 6 acres of rolling pasture land, beautiful woodlands and the babbling brook, which Bramble Beck is named after. The natural environment is their passion, so both on and around the park and surrounding farmland, there is an abundance of flora and fauna. They have also created their own arboretum for holiday makers to explore. Browse http://bramblebeckpark.com/ or telephone 01228 576615 for more information.

3. The Royal Oak has been a feature of the village for over 250 years old. They serve food and drink and once a week provide a fish & chip takeaway. For more information telephone 01228 576475 or browse their website at http://www.royaloakmoorhouse.co.uk/index.html.

Part 2 - Bus Stop Walks

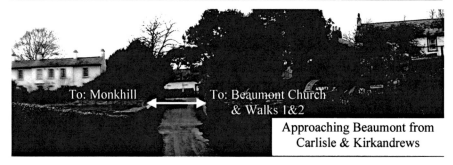

Carlisle - Beaumont

For bus times see page 10

	Title	Distance		Time	Page
		Miles	Km	Minutes	
1	Grinsdale - Beaumont along Hadrian's Trail	2.3	3.7	35	48
2	Grinsdale - Beaumont via Grinsdale Church and the estuary	3.3	5.4	50	49

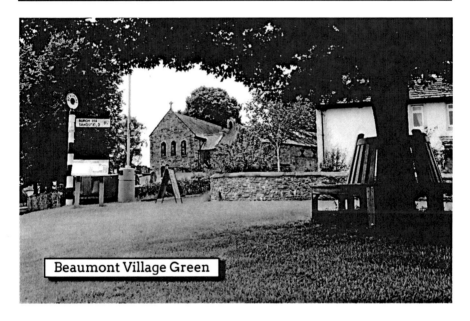

Beaumont Village Green

The Village Green at Beaumont is a convenient place to have a rest and a picnic - but please put your litter in the bin provided.

Hadrian's Wall Path (Walk 4 on page 52) continues along the Sandsfield road (see the signpost) .

The bus stop and Drover's Rest (see page 51) are on the other road past the Church and Walks 1 and 2 to Grinsdale are on the road that was behind the photographer when the above picture was taken.

Walk 1 : Grinsdale - Beaumont along Hadrian's Trail

Miles	Metres	OS Map	GPS	↓	↑	Remarks
		364 573	54.906362, -2.992828			The bus shelter is just off the main road
0.5	800					
		369 580	54.912483, -2.986293	Turn left	Turn right	This is the point where Hadrian's Wall Path meets the road. Follow the signs along the trail.
0.22	350					
		365 582	54.914119,-2.990909			The path passes a small copse of trees
0.29	470					
		361 581	54.913438, -2.998173			Bridge of Doudle Beck
0.49	785					
		355 584	54.916871, -3.008912			Kirkandrews

Hadrian's trails does not pass through Kirkandrews itself, but a short footpath links the trail with the village, where self-catering accommodation can be found at Hollow Creek. The old railway station and Kirkandrew's graveyard can also be found here - see page 12

Miles	Metres	OS Map	GPS	↓	↑	Remarks
0.64	1030					This is a beautiful part of the walk alongside the River Eden.
		350 594	54.925242, -3.015395	Turn left	Turn right	A farm road is reached. The walk continues into Beaumont
0.17	270					
		348 592	54.923756, -3.018729			Beamount

The bus stop is at the road junction, but just before it is reached is a public seat under cover of a tree where walkers can take a rest. The church is also here. See page 90

Walk 2 : Grinsdale - Beaumont via Grinsdale Church and the estuary

Miles	Metres	OS Map	GPS	↓	↑	Remarks
		364 573	54.906362, -2.992828			The bus shelter is just off the main road
0.5	800					
		369 580	54.912483, -2.986293	Straight on		This is the point where Hadrian's Wall Path meets the road but Walk 2 takes us through the village of Grinsdale
0.14	220					
		371 581	54.913692, -2.983483	Fork right	Left	The footpath leaves the farm road
0.15	240					
			54.913078, -2.981065			The Church is described on page 89. The walk continues along the banks of the River Eden in an unfenced field
1.98	3180					
		353 587	54.919723, -3.011598		Fork left	Rejoins the Hadrian's Wall Path and Walk 1 in a copse of trees.
0.41	660					
		350 594	54.925242, -3.015395	Turn left	Turn right	A farm road is reached. The walk continues into Beaumont
0.17	270					
		348 592	54.923756, -3.018729			Beamount

The bus stop is at the road junction, but just before it is reached is a public seat under cover of a tree where walkers can take a rest. The church is also here. See page 90

Beaumont - Burgh by Sands

	Title	Distance		Time	Page
		Miles	Km	Minutes	
1	Grinsdale - Beaumont along Hadrian's Trail	2.3	3.7	35	55
2	Grinsdale - Beaumont via Grinsdale Church and the estuary	3.3	5.4	50	56
3	Beaumont to The Drover's Rest	0.6	0.9	9	51
4	Beaumont to Burgh via Hadrian's Wall Path	1.3	2.1	20	52
5	Wormanby to Moorhouse	1.5	2/4	25	60

To Drovers Rest, Kirkandrews & Carlisle

To Burgh

To Beaumont

Drovers Rest

Monkhill

Walk 3 : Beaumont to the Drover's Rest

Miles	Metres	OS Map	GPS	↓	↑	Remarks
		348 592	, 54.923756, -3.0187299	Straight on		Beamount

The above co-ordinates are for the village green where a seat is provided for the weary walker. Here can be seen St. Mary's Church (page 90) . The bus stop is at the road junction.

Miles	Metres	OS Map	GPS	↓	↑	Remarks
0.4	590			Straight on		
		344 588	54.920105, -3.025070			The Roman Wall Lodges provide accommodation and are a 6 minute walk from the bus stop, but the bus will stop outside their gate upon request.
0.14	220					
		343 586	54.918174, -3.025809			The bus stops at the cross roads by request.

The stop is actually on the Beaumont road. Walk 3 has so far taken about 8 minutes and covered 0.8km or half a mile. Also here is the Methodist Chapel which serves as a community centre - see page 91. Please take your bearings from the signpost. The bus turns here as it travels between Burgh by Sands and Beaumont. The road to Moorhouse provides a short walk to catch the bus again. Walk 3 continues down the Kirkandrews road.

Miles	Metres	OS Map	GPS	↓	↑	Remarks
0.08	120					
		345 586	54.917977, -3.023914			The Drover's Rest

Total distance walked 0.9 km or 0.6 miles and has taken about 9 minutes.

For more information about accommodation at the Roman Wall Lodges and about the Drover's Rest - please see page 14

Walk 4 : Beaumont to Burgh via Hadrian's Wall Path

Miles	Metres	OS Map	GPS	↓	↑	Remarks
		348 592	54.923756, -3.018729	Right		Beaumount

The above co-ordinates are for the village green where a seat is provided for the weary walker. Here can be seen St. Mary's Church (page 90) . The bus stop is at the road junction.

Miles	Metres	OS Map	GPS	↓	↑	Remarks
0.1	120					This section along road
		348 594	54.924868, -3.018673	left	Right	Waymarked
0.9	1360					
		333 592	54.922498, -3.041464	left	Right	Greathill Beck
0.1	130					
		333 590	54.921371, -3.042184	Right	left	Main road

Walk 3 continues into Burgh by Sands, but at this point it is possible to walk in the opposite direction to the bridge at Wormanby and take Walk 5 to Moorhouse.- See page 53.

Miles	Metres	OS Map	GPS	↓	↑	Remarks
0.3	530					
		328 592	54.922351, -3.050169			Burgh by Sands

The total distance is 2.1 km or 1.3 miles and the time taken approximately 20 minutes.

The bus stop is outside St. Michael's Church - see page 92.

Walk 5 : Wormanby to Moorhouse

Miles	Metres	OS Map	GPS	↓	↑	Remarks
		334 589	54.920631, -3.040041			

The walk starts next to Wormanby Cottage and a footpath sign marks its location. The bus will not be able to stop on the bend but the driver, at his discretion may be able to stop before or after what used to be the old canal/railway bridge (now destroyed). Alternatively it is a very short walk from Burgh by Sands - see walk 4 on page 52.

Miles	Metres	OS Map	GPS	↓	↑	Remarks
1.1	1750	335 574	54.905801, -3.038783	Right	Left	The footpath meets the public highway
0.3	520					
		332 569	54.901593, -3.042177			T-Junction with Monkhill Road and the main road B5307
0.1	84			Left	Right	
			54.901344, -3.040929			Bus shelter/stop

The walk covers 2.4 km or 1.5 miles and takes about 25 minutes. At the T-Junction instead of turning for the Bus Shelter, it is suggested walking the same distance in the opposite direction to the Royal Oak, whilst waiting for the bus. If starting at Moorhouse, other public houses are available in Burgh or Monkhill.

Burgh by Sands - Dykesfield

A new statue to King Edward-I stands in the new recreation park.

Greyhound Inn

Bus stop

Monkhill

Drumburgh

Bus stop

Walk 7&8

Drumburgh

Monkhill

Walk 6 : Burgh - Edward-I's Monument - Old Sandsfield - Burgh

Miles	Metres	OS Map	GPS	↓	↑	Remarks
		329 592	54.922336, -3.050092			Bus stop next to Church

There are several bus stops in Burgh. This one is next to the Church. Start your walk by going towards Dykesfield and away from Monkhill. The route is waymarked/signposted.

Miles	Metres	OS Map	GPS	↓	↑	Remarks
0.02	34	328 592	54.922385, -3.050618	Right	Left	Cross Roads
0.7	1140	329 602	54.932475, -3.049032	Straight on		The footpath joins the public highway

The footpath we need is straight on, but it splits just after the public highway. The footpath heading east provides access to Burgh Marsh and from there Edward-I's monument can still be reached, but it is a slight detour

Miles	Metres	OS Map	GPS	↓	↑	Remarks
0.4	650	328 609	54.938223, -3.050849			Entry to Burgh Marsh from where the monument can be seen
0.1	200	326 609	54.938392, -3.054036			Edward-I's Monument.
0.6	1000					There no footpath, follow the hedge along the marsh towards the River Eden
		331 617	54.945125, -3.045551			Old Sandsfield

There is nothing left of the old Sandsfield port. A farmhouse marks its location. The farm itself is a working farm on private property so please do not trepass and invade the farmer's privacy.

This is the end of the public footpath and so we must retrace our steps back to Burgh.

The total length of the walk (there and back) is 4 miles or 6 kilometres and takes a minimum of one hour.

Walk 7 : Burgh - Longburgh and Dykesfield

Miles	Metres	OS Map	GPS	↓	↑	Remarks
		321 590	54.921120, -3.061771			Lawrence Lane Bus Stop see page 16
0.1	190					Walk down Lawrence Lane
		321 589	54.919715, -3.060570			The end of the public highway is site of the old

railway bridge. The station was on the east (Burgh side) of this road. The footpath continues through the gate but splits in two shortly after. Keep to the west branch.

Miles	Metres	OS Map	GPS	↓	↑	Remarks
0.3	550			Right	Left	
		318 585	54.916737, -3.066007	Right	Left	There is a T-junction of footpaths.
0.1	180					
		317 586	54.917952, -3.067883	Straight on		The footpath meets the public highway at a bend
0.03	50					Public highway
		317 586	54.918417, -3.068210	Left	Right	The footpath meets the public highway at a bend
0.3	510					Footpath
		312 586	54.917308, -3.075540			The footpath meets the public highway at a bend
0.3	500					Public highway
		308 589	54.920293, -3.080517			Longburgh. Straight on at the junction.
0.2	260					
		308 592	54.922383, -3.081546			Dykesfield

Total distance 1.4 miles (2.2 km) and takes about 25 minutes.

Walk 8 : Burgh - Thurstonfield

Miles	Metres	OS Map	GPS	↓	↑	Remarks
		321 590	54.921120, -3.061771			Lawrence Lane Bus Stop see page 16
0.1	190					Walk down Lawrence Lane
		321 589	54.919715, -3.060570			The end of the public highway is site of the old
						railway bridge. The station was on the east (Burgh side) of this road. The footpath continues through the gate but splits in two shortly after. Keep straight on.
0.2	290					
		318 585	54.917977, -3.057224	Straight on		The path turns almost a right angle and continues south
0.5	820					
		321 583	54.914406, -3.061315	Left	Right	T-Junction of footpaths
0.2	330					Footpath
		323 581	54.912374, -3.057565			Junction of footpath with minor road.
0.4	580					Minor road
		322 575	54.907459, -3.059486	Straight on		T-Junction of minor roads
						Minor road
0.6	1020	315 568	54.899741, -3.067957	Left	Right	Complex road junction in Thurstonfield
0	40					
		315 567	54.899561, -3.067406			The bus stop is on the main road near the telephone box

Total distance 1.8 miles (3 km) and takes about 30 minutes. The complex road junction in Thurstonfield is not as intimidating as it sounds since if the wrong road is taken, the Main Road is in view and the telephone box, near where the bus stops can easily be seen. Stand by the telephone box for journeys away from Carlisle and towards Kirkbride and on the opposite side of the road for journeys into Carlisle

Thurstonfield

Thurstonfield

Thurstonfield

End of Walk 8
Turn before this 'roundabout'

Walk 9 : Burgh - Dykesfield via Hadrian's Wall Path

The Hadrian's Wall Path between Burgh and Drumburgh follows the public highway used by the bus route.

Miles	Metres	OS Map	GPS	↓	↑	Remarks
0.5	760	328 592	54.922351, -3.050169			St Michael's Church Bus Stop
		321 590	54.921120, -3.061771			Lawrence Lane Bus Stop
Walk 9 carries straight on along the bus route. However, an alternative walk from here goes to Dykesfield - see Walk 7 on page 57 - and another one also goes down Lawrence Lane and ends up at Thurstonfield - see Walk 8 on page 58. The total time taken so far on Walk 9 is about 10 minutes.						
0.8	1300	308 592	54.922383, -3.081546			Dykesfield Bus Stop
This is the end of Walk 9 but it connects with other walks - see page 61. The total distance covered is about 1.3 miles (2.1km) and takes about 20 minutes.						

Most of Longburgh lies in a cul-de-sac off the Dykesfield - Thurstonfield Road

The entrance to Longburgh Pool

Dykesfield - Drumburgh

	Title	Distance		Time	Page
		Miles	Km	Minutes	
7	Burgh - Dykesfield	1.4	2.2	25	63
10A	Dykesfield - Boustead Hill	1.2	2	25	65
10A	Dykesfield - Haverlands	2.7	4.3	45	65
10B	Dykesfield - Easton	2.4	3.8	40	64
10B	Dykesfield - Finglandrigg	4	6.5	60	65
10C	Dykesfield - Drumburgh	2.7	4.3	45	65

The Hadrian's Wall would be parallel to the main road and pass through this building

Longburgh

Burgh   Drumburgh

Dykesfield

Longburgh is a pleasant hamlet (pictured on facing page) just a few yards down the road.

Drumburgh

Burgh

Walk 10 : Dykesfield - Drumburgh via Hadrian's Wall Path

The Hadrian's Wall Path between Burgh and Drumburgh follows the public highway used by the bus route. The walk can be split at Boustead Hill or Easton if required to see those hamlets that are located a short distance from the main road. Alternatively, the bus will stop on request near Boustead Hill or Easton to enable walkers to go through those hamlets to destinations on the Carlisle-Kirkbride road where the bus can be rejoined.

So the following pages provide some mix and match options.

- **Dykesfield to Drumburgh** Walk 10 (described at the beginning of walks 10A,B and C)

- **Dykesfield to Boustead Hill** Walk 10A

- **Dykesfield to Havelands** Walk 10A

- **Boustead Hill to Havelands** Walk 10A

- **Dykesfield to Easton** Walk 10B

- **Dykesfield to Finglandrigg** Walk 10B

- **Easton to Finglandrigg** Walk 10B

- **Easton to Drumburgh** Walk 10C Do this walk in the reverse direction to start at Drumburgh and end up at any of the above destinations.

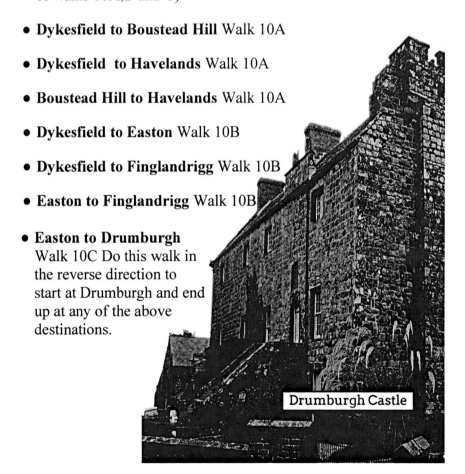

Drumburgh Castle

Walk 10A : Dykesfield - Boustead Hill - Haverlands

Miles	Metres	OS Map	GPS	↓	↑	Remarks
		308 592	54.922383, -3.081546			Dykesfield Bus Stop
0.8	1300					
		295 594	54.923849, -3.101734	Left	Right	Road Junction The bus stops here by request
Walk 10 to Drumburgh continues straight on as Walk 10B on page 64. The walk has taken about 20 minutes from Dykesfield						
0.1	150					
		295 592	54.922500, -3.102210			Highfield Farm B&B is a 2 minute walk from bus stop see page 18
0.3	490					Keep to the public highway, which has a couple of sharp bends
		292 589	54.919930, -3.106453			Boustead Hill Equestrian Centre - see page 18.
The Equestrian Centre is the last place in Boustead Hill and has taken about 6 minutes to walk the 650 metres (0.4 miles) from the bus stop. The road continues to Haverlands, where the bus may be rejoined along the Havelands Straight.						
1.5	2370					
		291 569	54.901640, -3.107670			Haverlands Layby
The bus does not normally stop at Haverlands Layby, situated between Kirkbampton and Finglandrigg so please look conspicuous. The distance from the Boustead Hill Bus stop is 3km (1.9 miles) and will take about 30 minutes to walk. The distance from Dykesfield is 4.3 km (2.7 miles) and would take about 45 minutes to walk.						

Walk 10B : Dykesfield - Easton - Finglandrigg

Miles	Metres	OS Map	GPS	↓	↑	Remarks
1.2	1930	295 594	54.923849, -3.101734	Straight on		Road Junction see Walk 10A
		276 596	54.926066, -3.131733	Left	Right	Road Junction. The bus stops here by request.

Walk 10 to Drumburgh continues straight on as Walk 10C on page 65
The walk has taken about 30 minutes so far

Miles	Metres	OS Map	GPS	↓	↑	Remarks
0.4	590					
		277 591	54.920879, -3.130066			Midtown Farm B&B is in the centre of Easton see page 18

Midtown Farm is about 5 minutes walk from the bus stop and from Dykesfield it is 2.4 miles (3.8 km) and has taken about 40 minutes.

The public highway continues to Finglandrigg

Miles	Metres	OS Map	GPS	↓	↑	Remarks
1.3	2060					
		278 574	54.905707, -3.127335			Road Junction with the Kirkbride-Kirkbampton road (B5307), which is the bus route
	610					
		283 571	54.903531, -3.118634			Finglandrigg National Nature Reserve

Total Distance from Dykesfield 6.5 km or 4 miles and takes about one hour to walk. The total distance from the Easton Lane End Bus stop is 3.3 km (2 miles) and takes about 30 minutes.

Finglandrigg

Walk 10B to Easton

to Finglandrigg Wood & Carlisle

To Fingland & Kirkbride

Walk 10C : Dykesfield - Drumburgh

Miles	Metres	OS Map	GPS	↓	↑	Remarks
		276 596	54.926066, -3.131733			Road Junction. See Walk 10B
0.7	1090					
		277 591	54.927258, -3.148653			Drumburgh

Total Distance from Dyksfield to Drumburgh 4.3 km (2.7 miles) and takes about 45 minutes

The old railway station can be seen on the approach to Drumburgh

Easton Lane End

Drumburgh - Glasson

	Title	Distance		Time	Page
		Miles	Km	Minutes	
10A	Dykesfield - Boustead Hill	1.2	2	25	65
10A	Dykesfield - Haverlands	2.7	4.3	45	65
10B	Dykesfield - Easton	2.4	3.8	40	64
10B	Dykesfield - Finglandrigg	4	6.5	60	65
10C	Dykesfield - Drumburgh	2.7	4.3	45	65
11	Drumburgh - Dykesfield via Hadrian's Wall Path	4	6.5	60	67
11A 10B	Drumburgh - Easton	1	1.7	15	67 65
11A 10B	Drumburgh - Finglandrigg	2.7	4.4	45	67 65
10C 10B 10A	Drumburgh - Boustead Hill	2.3	3.7	35	65 63
12	Drumburgh - Kirkbride via Drumburgh Moss	3.3	5.3	50	68
13	Drumburgh-Glasson via Hadrian's Wall Path	1.5	2.5	25	70

Drumburgh

Walk 11 : Drumburgh - Dykesfield via Hadrian's Wall Path

The Hadrian's Wall Path between Burgh and Drumburgh follows the public highway used by the bus route.

Walk 11A : Drumburgh - Easton

Miles	Metres	OS Map	GPS	↓	↑	Remarks
0.7	1090	277 591	54.927258, -3.148653			Drumburgh
		276 596	54.926066, -3.131733	Right	Left	Road Junction. See Walk 10B The bus stops here by request
The walk to Dykesfield carries straight on at the above road junction, and is described in Walk 11B, but Walk 11A goes to Easton and follows the same route as Walk 10B on page 64 The walk from Drumburgh has taken about 10 minutes to this point. After Easton Walk 10B continues to Finglandrigg						

Walk 11B : Drumburgh - Boustead Hill

Miles	Metres	OS Map	GPS	↓	↑	Remarks
1.2	1930	276 596	54.926066, -3.131733			Walk 11A
		295 594	54.923849, -3.101734	Right	Left	See Walk 11C The bus stops here by request
The walk to Dykesfield carries straight on at the above road junction, and is described in Walk 11C, but Walk 11B goes to Boustead Hill and follows the same route as Walk 10A on page 63 The walk from Drumburgh has taken about 30 minutes to this point and has covered about 1.9 miles ((3 km) After Boustead Hill Walk 10A continues to Haverlands Layby						

Walk 11C : Drumburgh - Dyksfield

Miles	Metres	OS Map	GPS	↓	↑	Remarks
0.8	1300	295 594	54.923849, -3.101734			See Walk 11B The bus stops here by request
		308 592	54.922383, -3.081546			Dykesfield Bus Stop
Total Distance from Drumburgh is 6.5 km or 4 miles and takes about one hour to walk.						

Walk 12 : Drumburgh - Kirkbride via Drumburgh Moss

Miles	Metres	OS Map	GPS	↓	↑	Remarks
		277 591	54.927258, -3.148653			Drumburgh
The bus stops at a T Junction. Walk 12 proceeds down the minor road.						
0.5	880	259 592	54.922383, -3.157506	Straight on		T Junction of footpaths
The path is next to the old railway track from Silloth/Kirkbride to Drumburgh/Carlisle. The Romans also used this path to carry supplies from their fort in Kirkbride (on the site of Kirkbride Church) to their fort at Drumburgh. At this point the walk is on the Drumburgh Moss National Nature Reserve (see page 110) and provides open access, but walking is far easier if the waymarked footpaths are used.						
0.2	250	258 592	54.921365, -3.160903			Moss Cottage is a private dwelling and not part of the NNR
0.4	620	251 589	54.919130, -3.169201	Straight on		A private footpath to Whiteholme joins here. Whiteholme used to be a chemical works. Our path is a lower quality
0.1	180	250 588	54.918139, -3.171456	Straight on		The public footpath leaves the NNR and continues on private land of higher quality.
0.2	290	249 586	54.916018, -3.173151	Right	Left	The public footpath returns to the NNR on a winding path of lower quality.
0.2	300	246 586	54.915889, -3.177418	Straight on		The public footpath leaves the NNR and enters the parish of Aikton. It is now a recognisable lane.
0.5	850	241 579	54.910507, -3.186781	Straight on		Junction of footpath with public highway

Miles	Metres	OS Map	GPS	↓	↑	Remarks
		241 579	54.910507, -3.186781	Straight on		Junction of footpath with public highway
0.2	350					Greenspot - Whitrigg Road
0.7	1090		54.911771, -3.191494	Left	Right	The River Wampool is crossed by a footbridge. The public footpath across Kirkbride Marsh is subject to tidal flooding - see page 117
0.3	550	229 574	54.906298, -3.204663	Left	Right	Junction of Public Footpath with Public Highway. Kirkbride/Aikton Parish boundary
						Whitrigg- Kirkbride road, passing the entrance to Cumbria Turf.
		228 569	54.901657, -3.203627			Bus stop outside the Bush Public House.

The Bush offers a pleasant place to wait for the bus as it offers food, drink and customer toilets. The total distance covered by this walk is 3.3 miles (5.3km) and takes about 50 minutes to complete.

Kirkbride Village Hall   To: Whitrigg, Anthorn & Bowness   To: Church   Bush Inn,

Walk 13 : Drumburgh - Glasson via Hadrian's Wall Path

Miles	Metres	OS Map	GPS	↓	↑	Remarks
		277 591	54.927258, -3.148653			Drumburgh
The bus stops at a T Junction. Walk 12 proceeds down the minor road.						
0.5	880					
		259 592	54.922383, -3.157506	Right	Left	T Junction of footpaths
The path that goes straight on is Walk 12 on page 68						
0.4	640					Hadrian's Wall Path
		254 596	54.922383, -3.157506			Walker House (Private Dwelling)
0.2	390					
		253 600	54.928970, -3.166370	Left	Right	The path turns a right angle
160ft	50					
			54.928896, -3.167087	Right	Left	The path turns a right angle
0.3	430					
		251 604	54.932203, -3.170173	Right	Left	Junction of footpath with Glasson-Whitrigg Road
330ft	100					Hadrian's Wall Path goes through the middle of Glasson
		252 604	54.932917, -3.169207			Glasson Bus Stop / Shelter

The total distance travelled is about 1.5 miles (2.5 km) and takes about 25 minutes.

Whilst waiting for the next bus, the Highland Laddie, further up the village, offers food, drink and customer toilets.

Glasson - Port Carlisle

	Title	Distance		Time	Page
		Miles	Km	Minutes	
13	Drumburgh-Glasson via Hadrian's Wall Path	1.5	2.5	25	70
14	Glasson - Port Carlisle	1.7	2.7	30	74

Glasson

The Highland Laddie, Glassson

Walk 14 : Glasson - Port Carlisle via Hadrian's Wall Path

Miles	Metres	OS Map	GPS	↓	↑	Remarks
		252 604	54.932917, -3.169207			Glasson Bus Stop / Shelter
0.1	180					Public Highway
		253 606	54.934165, -3.167312	Left	Right	Cross roads by Highland Laddie Inn. Hadrian's Wall Path is waymarked
0.6	980					
		246 612	54.939936, -3.178631	Right	Left	Entrance to Cottage and Glendale Holiday Park.

A restaurant with customer toilets is available in the Holiday Park. Walk 14 continues to Port Carlisle. Walk 15 also passes the entrance to the Holiday Park between the bus stop and Glasson Moss Nature Reserve.

Miles	Metres	OS Map	GPS	↓	↑	Remarks
0.1	160					
		247 613	54.941078, -3.177344	Left	Right	Request Bus Stop at this T Junction. Hadrian's Wall Path continues in wooded area between the road and the Solway
0.6	990					
		241 622	54.948520, -3.185025			The old Harbour at Port Carlisle.

Pause here to take a selfie in front of a space-time signpost. Two arms of which show the distance and direction of the two ends of Hadrian's Wall, (Bowness and Wallsend), in a conventional manner, whilst a third arm records today's date that is updated by its owner, Mr Roger Brough who may upon request add a fourth arm customised to the tourists home town.

Miles	Metres	OS Map	GPS	↓	↑	Remarks
0.2	300					
		239 623	54.949686, -3.188740			Junction with Bowness-Glasson Road. Hadrian's Wall Path continues straight on to Bowness along the public highway
440 ft	140					
		240 623	54.948712, -3.187485			Hope and Anchor, Port Carlisle

Total distance 1.7 miles (2.7km) and takes about 30 minutes to walk.

Port Carlisle - Bowness on Solway

	Title	Distance		Time	Page
		Miles	Km	Minutes	
14	Glasson - Port Carlisle	1.7	2.7	30	72
15	Port Carlisle - Bowness via Hadrian's Wall Path	1.2	2	20	74
16	Port Carlisle - Bowness via Brackenrigg	2.3	3.7	35	77

Port Carlisle

Port Carlisle

Walk 15 : Port Carlisle - Bowness via Hadrian's Wall Path

Miles	Metres	OS Map	GPS	↓	↑	Remarks
		240 623	54.948712, -3.187485			Hope and Anchor, Port Carlisle
440 ft	140					
		239 623	54.949686, -3.188740			Walk 15 joins Hadrian's Wall Path at the point were Walk 14 leaves it.
1	1620					Hadrian's Wall Path follows the public highway
		225 624	54.953935, -3.211776	Left	Right	Follow the way marked signs as Hadrian's Wall Path leaves the public highway
0.1	170					
		223 623	54.953935, -3.211776			Hadrian's Wall Path terminates on a promenade overlooking the estuary
210 ft	65					
		223 623	54.953456, -3.212859	Right	Left	Our walk ends on the public highway.

The walk from Port Carlisle covered a total of 1.2 miles (2 km) and took about 20 minutes.

The village of Bowness has few places where residents can park their cars and the bus sometimes has difficulty negotiating the narrow road. Consequently, the bus may be unable to stop exactly on its designated place due to parked cars. The landlord of the King's Arms will be happy to advise the best place to stand. Better still, take some refreshment in the King's Arms while you wait. Walk in the opposite direction (towards Port Carlisle) to reach Shoregate House and the Old Chapel, both establishments providing accommodation. Wallsend Guest House, The Lindow Hall (providing bunk-bed accommodation) and St. Michael's Church are a short walk down the road that joins this road at the King;s Arms -see page 28 for details.

Walk 16 : Port Carlisle - Bowness via Brackenrigg

Miles	Metres	OS Map	GPS	↓	↑	Remarks
		240 623	54.948712, -3.187485			Hope and Anchor, Port Carlisle. Turn right after leaving pub.
0.2	290					Public highway Port Carlisle-Glasson
		242 611	54.946627, -3.184878	Right	Left	Former Methodist Chapel
0.4	570					Public footpath
0.5	790	238 618	54.944209, -3.190717	Left	Right	From the Port Carlisle Direction, the footpath makes a turn to the right, then, after 547 feet (167 m) at the point marked by these coordinates, there is a T-junction of footpaths.
0.1	190	232 614	54.941512, -3.201389	Right	Left	Brackenrigg, private farm buildings
0.2	360	230 615	4.942545, -3.203850	Left	Right	The correct path seems obvious at this T-junction.
0.8	1330	227 614	54.940988, -3.208489	Right	Left	T-junction of footpath with Bowness-Whitrigg public highway
		224 626	54.951866, -3.213154	Straight on		Wallsend Guest House
300 ft	90			|		Public highway
		223 626	54.952354, -3.214315	Straight on		St. Michael's Church
270 ft	80					Public highway
		223 627	54.952354, -3.214315	Right	Left	King's Arms

Total distance 2.3 miles (3.7 km) and takes about 35 minutes to walk.

Bowness on Solway - Cardurnock

	Title	Distance		Time	Page
		Miles	Km	Minutes	
15	Port Carlisle - Bowness via Hadrian's Wall Path	1.2	2	20	74
16	Port Carlisle - Bowness via Brackenrigg	2.3	3.7	35	77
†	Bowness - Bowness Nature Reserve	1.2	2	20	
†	Bowness - West Common	1.7	2.8	25	
†	Bowness - Campfield	1.8	2.9	30	
17	Campfield - Longcroft	3.5	5.7	55	
†	Bowness - Cardurnock	4.3	6.9	65	
18	Cardurnock- Cardurnock Moss	1.5	3.7	25	81
†	Cardurnock - Anthorn				

† via public highway (no further description required)

Campfield Nature Reserve

West Common

Campfield Nature Reserve
marked by a sign
travelling from Anthorn

Campfield Nature Reserve
around corner travelling
from Bowness

Walk 17 : Campfield - Anthorn

Miles	Metres	OS Map	GPS	↓	↑	Remarks
		199 584	54.924529, -3.248429			There are two bus stops in Anthorn. This one is at The Island and has a bus shelter.
0.3	530					Walk along the road in the direction of the Radio Station
		195 582	54.912224, -3.257491	Right	Left	Anthorn Bridge
0.1	250					
		195 584	54.914435, -3.257868	Right	Left	Junction of footpaths
0.4	620					
		199 588	54.917555, -3.249907	Left	Right	Junction of footpaths
0.4	660					
		197 595	54.923231, -3.253220	Right	Left	Junction of footpaths.

About 110 ft (34 metres) before this point the terrain becomes rougher on the Bowness Common NNR. Our walk departs slightly from the public footpath to avoid crossing a farmer's field and our walk is easier to navigate.

Miles	Metres	OS Map	GPS	↓	↑	Remarks
0.2	350					
		201 596	54.924690, -3.248254	Fork Left	Right	Junction of footpaths. Going straight is also possible. Turn left when you reach the larger footpath, then fork right.
0.3	470					
		202 601	54.928680, -3.246682			Junction of Walks 17 and 19 This is on the Campfield Marsh Nature Reserve- see page 80

At this point you have the option to join Walk 17A for Rogersceugh and Longcroft.

Miles	Metres	OS Map	GPS	↓	↑	Remarks
0.6	930					
		201 608	54.935295, -3.248161	Left	Right	Hides for public use are just off this walk
0.6	910					
		197 616	54.942590, -3.254477			Campfield. Entrance to RSPB Reserve. Request Bus Stop

Total distance 3.2 miles (5.2 km) and takes about 50 minutes to walk.

Walk 18 :Cardurnock - Cardurnock Moss

Wellington boots are required as the lonning can be very muddy. Unlike the rest of the walks in this book, this one is there and back with no other bus stop to link it to.

Miles	Metres	OS Map	GPS	↓	↑	Remarks
			54.917130, -3.292651			The Horse and Jockey is now a private dwelling. Walk away from the radio station.
180 ft	60					Public Highway
			54.917579, -3.292241	Right	Left	Cardurnock Pond - now drained
0.7	1130					Public footpath. The gate marks the boundary of the Nature Reserve, which is open to the public .
			54.920094, -3.275385			Cardurnock Moss is part of Bowness Common.

It is possible to continue the walk across this open land but the terrain is wet and difficult. For more information see page 114.

Total distance 1.5 miles (3.7 km) and takes about 25 minutes to walk.

Cardurnock Pond

Approaching Cardurnock from Bowness

Anthorn - Kirkbride

	Title	Distance		Time	Page
		Miles	Km	Minutes	
†	Cardurnock - Anthorn	3.2	5.2	50	
17	Anthorn - Campfield	3.2	5.2	50	85
†	Anthorn - Longcroft	1.2	2	20	
19	Longcroft - Campfield	3.5	5.7	55	77
†	Longcroft - Whitrigg	1.2	2	20	
†	Whitrigg - Kirkbride	1.7	2.8	25	
†	Anthorn - Kirkbride	1.8	2.9	30	
†	Cardurnock - Cardurnock Marsh				

† via public highway (no further description required)

There are two bus stops in Anthorn

Anthorn Bridge

Walk 19 :Campfield - Longcroft

Miles	Metres	OS Map	GPS	↓	↑	Remarks
		197 616	54.942590, -3.254477			Campfield. Entrance to RSPB Reserve. Request Bus Stop
0.6	910					
		201 608	54.935295, -3.248161	Right	Left	Hides for public use are just off this walk
0.6	930					
		202 601	54.928680, -3.246682	Fork Left	Right	Junction of Walks 17 and 19 - see page 77

Journey time so far is 1.4 miles or 2.3 km 22 minutes

Miles	Metres	OS Map	GPS	↓	↑	Remarks
0.9	1400					This is a winding footpath. Other paths are available.
		214 597	54.925567, -3.227677	Left	Right	Junction of footpath with driveway
0.2	250					
		216 598	54.926639, -3.224919			Rogersceugh

Rogersceugh Farm is now owned by the RSPB. Wildlife can be observed from its barn. This walk is 2.5 miles (4km) from Campfield and has taken about 40 minutes. You have the option to return to Campfield or continue to Longcroft. In either case we need to retrace our steps to the junction of the footpath.

Miles	Metres	OS Map	GPS	↓	↑	Remarks
0.2	250					
		214 597	54.925567, -3.227677	Left	Right	Junction of footpath with driveway
0.9	1500					
		217 582	54.912384, -3.223351	Left	Right	Junction of driveway with public highway. This is on a corner, please walk a little way to enable to bus to stop safely.

Total distance 3.5 miles (5.7 km) and takes about 55 minutes to walk.

Kirkbride - Kirkbampton

	Title	Distance		Time	Page
		Miles	Km	Minutes	
†	Kirkbride bus stop - Midtown Stores	0.1	0.2	2	
†	Kirkbride bus stop - old Station	0.3	0.5	5	
†	Kirkbride Bus Stop - The Bush	0.5	0.9	8	
	Kirkbride - walk 20	2.4	3.9	40	87
†	Kirkbride - Fingland bus stop	2.2	3.5	35	
†	Kirkbride to Finglandrigg Wood	3.9	6.3	60	
†	Kirkbride - Kirkbampton bus stop	5.5	8.9	85	

† via public highway (no further description required)

Kirkbride Bus Stop

The old Railway Bridge   Bus turns at this road junction

Old School - Kirkbride - another bus stop

Walk 20 : Kirkbride Church - Kirkbride School

Miles	Metres	OS Map	GPS	↓	↑	Remarks
		228 569	54.901657, -3.203627			Bus stop outside the Bush Public House. On leaving The Bush, turn right.
140 ft	40					
		228 569	54.902170, -3.203567			Two lanes join the main road. Walk up Church Road.
0.2	360					
		229 574	54.904444, -3.203318	Straight on		St. Bride's Church
270 ft	80					
		231 574	54.904864, -3.202597	The public highway ends but the footpath is straight on.		
0.3	480					
		231 574	54.905098, -3.200373	Right	Left	Footpath junction
0.2	230					
				Left	Right	Junction with Birch Hill Lane

At this point we are 0.2 miles (270 metres) from the junction near the Bush. You can save 8 minutes walk time by missing out the Church part of this walk.

Miles	Metres	OS Map	GPS	↓	↑	Remarks
0.2	330					
		225 572	54.903547, -3.194667	Right	Left	Junction with main Kirkbride-Carlisle Road through gate

The area that is concreted is the track of the old railway.

Miles	Metres	OS Map	GPS	↓	↑	Remarks
220 ft	70					Kirkbride-Carlisle Road (B5307)
		235 571	54.903127, -3.195249	Left	Right	Junction of footpath with main road

Miles	Metres	OS Map	GPS	↓	↑	Remarks
		235 571	54.903127, -3.195249	Left	Right	Junction of footpath with main road
0.3	470					
		234 568	54.899785, -3.195096	Left	Right	Cross roads of footpaths

All footpaths go to Kirkbride and join the main road at various places. The path that leads straight on from this point passes the Kirkbride Sewage Works - which has little of interest to the tourist! The path described here takes the more interesting route of this network of paths.

Miles	Metres	OS Map	GPS	↓	↑	Remarks
0.2	260					
		236 565	54.897824, -3.193089	Right	Left	Junction of paths
0.1	200					
		236 565	54.896494, -3.195192	Straight on		Junction of paths
0.2	250					
		232 563	54.895631, -3.198763	Left	Right	Cross roads of footpaths
0.3	550					Ignore any other footpaths until almost opposite an old hangar.
		234 558	54.891010, -3.196173	Right	Left	Junction of paths
0.1	230					
			54.890653, -3.199755	Right	Left	Junction of main road and footpath near old hangar
0.3	450					
		229 562	54.894277, -3.202893	Left	Right	Bus stop at Beech Lea by the school.

Total Distance 2.4 miles (3.9 km) and takes about 40 minutes

Kirkbampton - Carlisle

	Title	Distance		Time	Page
		Miles	Km	Minutes	
†	Kirkbampton Bus stop - Thurstonfield	0.4	0.6	6	
†	Kirkbampton - Thurdsonfield Chapelfield Lane	0.5	0.9	8	
†	Kirkbampton - Thurstonfield Lough	0.7	1.1	11	
†	Kirkbampton - Moor Park/Bramble Beck	0.9	1.4	15	
†	Kirkbampton - Moorhouse Royal Oak	1.6	2.5	25	
†	Kirkbampton - Moorhouse Bus Stop	1.7	2.9	26	

† via public highway (no further description required)

Moorhouse

	Title	Distance		Time	Page
		Miles	Km	Minutes	
†	Moorhouse Bus stop - Carlisle Bus Station	4.5	7.3	70	

† via public highway (no further description required)

Part 3 - The Peninsular Story

The Romans

There has been so much written about Hadrian's Wall and the Romans in this part of the country that to include it all would overwhelm this book. Therefore, this chapter is only a basic guide to understand what we see through the bus windows or on the walks described elsewhere in this book. Of course nothing remains to be seen of the Roman occupation but if we view the landscape surrounding the sites of interest we may appreciate its strategic location. The GPS coordinates given here are only approximate.

Carlisle to Beaumont

1. **Carlisle. Uxelodunum also known as Petriana** The Roman fort was at Stanwix, which can not be seen from the Bus, but was located just north of the Eden Bridge on the northern bank of the Eden. It was the largest fort on Hadrian's Wall but nothing remains of it today.

Beaumont to Burgh by Sands

2. Beaumont Parish Church is on the site of Turret 70A - see page 90.

Burgh by Sands to Dykesfield

3. **Burgh by Sands** the Romans called it **Aballava.** The fort was strategically placed to garrison the guards of two important crossing points on the Solway, Peatwath and Sandwath. Aballava, meaning 'Orchard' in Latin, was 4000 ft (120m) east to west and 500 ft(150m) north to south. Other forts in Burgh have been found that pre-date Hadrian's Wall

4. Turret 72B is on private land but close to the footpath that leads to Watch Hill, some 21 metres above sea level. (GPS 54.923215, -3.071558)

5. Milecastle 73 is in the same private field about 500 metres to the west. Its location approximates to a farmer's barn see page 61. (GPS 54.923707, -3.079882).

Dykesfield to Drumburgh

6. Milecastle 76 was just outside the fort at Coggabata. Along Burgh Marsh the highest tides would wash up against the wall. (GPS54.928309, -3.143864)

Drumburgh to Glasson

7. **Drumburgh** the Romans called it **Coggabata.** The small hill on which the fort was built provided a commanding view of two important crossing points on the Solway, Stonewath and Sandwath. Supplies to the fort were via the Stanegate to Kirkbride. Stanegate, a stone road built by the Romans before the Wall and linked Carlisle with Corbridge. The extension between Drumburgh and Kirkbride can be followed in part on Walk 12,(see page 68) which is also the track taken by the railway.

8. Milecastle 77 was located adjacent to the modern roadway. Its elevation of about 14 metres would have given an excellent panorama of the estuary. (GPS 54.934870, -3.161305). A public footpath at the Glasson Lane End road junction leads to a high point of 18 metres but I am not sure if the Romans took advantage of this.

Glasson to Port Carlisle

9. Milecastle 78 is located very close to the entrance to the Caravan Park. In fact just on the Port Carlisle side of the entrance are a series of wooden outbuildings in a private field close to the road. These are almost on the site of the milecastle. (GPS 54.941078, -3.178939)

10. Turret 78A was located on the bend in the road on the Port Carlisle side of Kirkland House. (GPS 54.944900, -3.183433)

Port Carlisle to Bowness

11. Milecastle 79 is marked by a farmer's barn across the field from the 30mph speed limit sign. (GPS 54.948909, -3.194923)

12. Turret 79B, the last turret before Maia, has no landmark features but is located in the middle of a private field. (GPS 54.951441, -3.206616

Bowness to Cardurnock

13. **Bowness. Maia** The Roman fort, meaning 'larger' was the second largest fort on Hadrian's Wall and built on the site of Milecastle 80 Covering 7 acres the fort measured 710ft (220m) by 420 ft (130m). Its granary was thought to be on the site of St. Michael's Church.

Cardurnock to Kirkbride

14. **Cardurnock. The fort near the Pebbly Place.** It is unknown what the Romans called it but would have monitored any shipping trying to enter Moricambe Bay behind the fortifications. The location provides a clear view of the Solway from Silloth, across to the mountain called Criffel and the Dumfriesshire coast.

15. The fortifications continued down the west coast of Cumbria to Silloth and Maryport

16. **Kirkbride** predates Hadrian's Wall and was built on the site of St. Bride's Church in the time of the Emperor Agricola. It provided the western end of the Stanegate frontier linking Carlisle with Corbridge. It is thought that Portus Trucculensis was a port on Moricambe Bay by means of which supplies could be imported from Rome and elsewhere. The fort measured 525 ft (160m) x 495 ft (150m)

Methodist Chapel, Bowness

Church History

In the previous chapter the Roman Wall and its history was discussed. No mention was made of a theory suggesting that the father of St Patrick, the patron saint of Ireland, was a Roman soldier stationed on Hadrian's Wall. It is thought that Patrick was born at Birdoswald (one of the forts on the Wall between Carlisle and Hexham), and if true we might speculate that as a boy he made the journey along the Wall with his father between Carlisle and Bowness - just as the 93 Bus does today. OK it may be a speculative thought but it leads poetically into this section on the Churches on the Peninsular.

St. Kentigern's Church, Grinsdale

A church was built here in the 12th century. Hugh de Morville of Appleby gave the Church to Lanercost Priory. The church fell into disrepair and the present church was built on its site in about 1740 at the expense of Joseph Dacre and was restored in 1895. The church is not on the bus route but is featured on Walk 2 on page 49.

St. Mary's Beaumont

The bus stop (page 14) is opposite St Mary's Church and is an example of 'swords into ploughshares' as it was on this site that the Romans built Turret 70A on Hadrian's Wall to take advantage of the commanding view of the Solway and guard the nearby crossing of the Solway that the cattle drovers used in later years. In the 12th century the Normans built a small castle here. It became a church in 1296 when Sir Elias de Thirwall was its first Rector. Little remains of the original church except perhaps the south doorway and the three east windows. The other windows, porch and vestry were restored in the 19th century. Other additions and restorations were made in 1784, 1872 and 1888. During the restorations in Victorian times, two medieval grave slabs were discovered and these are built into the west wall behind the font. The congregation includes those who live in Kirkandrews as their church no longer exists, its location marked by the graveyard. The church is now in the spiritual care of the Rector of Burgh-by-Sands.

Monkhill Methodist Chapel

Just seven members of the Burgh-by-Sands Methodist Society met in people homes in 1838 with services led by local preachers and travelling preachers based at the Fisher Street Wesleyan Chapel that had opened in Carlisle in 1817. Membership increased and by 1841 the society was known as Burgh and Kirkandrews, then in 1846 simply as Kirkandrews. The foundation stone for the Monkhill Chapel was laid on 20 May 1858 after the land had been acquired for £5 and the society was renamed the Monkhill Wesleyan Society. The building, which had a capacity for 75 worshippers was too small for the growing membership. The present building was opened on 27 October 1904 after additional land had been acquired and provides not only a place of worship for a congregation of 120, but a schoolroom, vestry storeroom etc. More recent modifications provide wheelchair access, toilets and an improved kitchen that provides a monthly "Lunch with Us" for parishioners and friends. The chapel is open daily for walkers, cyclists and campers.

St Michael's Burgh-by-Sands

It is not often that a church is fortified, but this church, together with its rectory was fortified against attacks from Scotland, notably the Border Reivers. Similar fortifications were incorporated in the nearby church at Newton Arlosh. St. Michael's Burgh was built in the 12th century on the site of Aballava, the Roman fort, and formed part of Hadrian's Wall. The north doorway dates from Norman times as do many other features in the church.

The battlemented West Tower probably dates from the middle of the 14th century. Arrow slits form the windows and a narrow iron-gated doorway, (known as a yett), restricts access to the pele tower. The church was altered in 1713 and restored in 1881.

It was here that King Edward-I lay in state (see page 97). The churchyard path features a time-line, made from granite, that depicts significant historical events.

St. Michael's, Bowness-on-Solway

St. Michael's Church is built on the site of the Roman Granary within the Maia Fort. In the 12th century the Normans used the stones of the fort in its construction. The beautifully carved font also dates from Norman times although it is supported on a shaft dating from 1848. Remnants of the Norman architecture can be seen on the doorways that are located on the north and south sides of the Church. The windows date from Victorian times except for the one on the north side, which is Norman. In 1891 the North Transept was added. Outside the church, the sundial is from the 18th century. The bells that now ring in the belfry are not those taken from Dornock and Middlebie churches, these are proudly displayed in the porch - see page 28. The Old Rectory is now the Wallsend Guest House. A new rectory was built next door but this too is in private hands as the pastoral care of the parish is now under the Rector of Kirkbride.

Bowness Methodist Chapel

The Wesleyan Home Mission Chapel was built in Bowness in 1872 by William Topping of Bowness and provided seating for a congregation of 50. It closed in the 1980's and now provides self-catering accommodation - see page 28.

St. Bride's Kirkbride

St. Bride's church, after which the village is named, can not be seen easily from the bus, but is a short walk away from *The Bush* - see walk 19 - page 82. Brocca, the mother of St. Bride, was baptised by St. Patrick and as a boy Patrick may well have visited this area as it is thought his father, Calpurnius, was stationed on Hadrian's Wall and at another time down the coast at what is now Ravenglass. Brigid was born about 451 and became Abbess of Kildare and one of the patron saints of Ireland. The church was built in 1189 on the site of the Roman fort and was linked to their fort at Drumburgh by a road the path of which is followed (more or less) on Walk 12 - page 68. A guide book, which gives more information about the church is available from the church or browse http://www.kirkbridecommunity.co.uk/

Kirkbride Hill, Primative Methodist Chapel

The first chapel was built in Kirkbride in 1866 but was demolished about 1905 to make way for a new chapel on the same site. It had a chapel measuring 52ft x 24 ft, a schoolroom 24ft x 14ft and a vestry 8ft x 10ft. Since 1963 it has been a private residence as the congregation merged with Kirkbride Midtown. It is situated near the Old School.

Kirkbride Midtown, Wesleyan Methodist Chapel

Four years after the building of the Primitive Methodist Chapel, the Wesleyan Methodists built their own chapel to house a congregation of 100. The chapel was 21ft x 29.5ft and schoolroom 28.5ft x 22ft. It closed in 1992 is now a private residential building.

St Peter's Kirkbampton

The Normans built this church in 1194 as evidence of the Norman doorway and beautifully carved chancel arch. Stone to build the church was recycled from the Roman occupation and stone in the south wall bears a Latin inscription that translated means "The troops of the 6th Legion, the victorious, pious and faithful, did this work". A carved stone of Roman origin was revealed when plaster-work was removed in the 1870 restoration of the church. The two bells that are used today were cast in 1705.

Thurstonfield Methodist Chapel

Farmer Thomas Stordy sold the land on which stands Thurstonfield Methodist Chapel for £5. The Wesleyan chapel opened in September 1861 and was attached to the Carlisle-based circuit. In 1911 the Sunday School and Vestry were built. The entrance porch dates from 1994. Until 1998 a cinder track provided access, then the adjacent housing development required this to be upgraded to a tarmac road and at that time the interior of the chapel was refurbished.

King Edward I

King Edward-I, also known as Edward Longshanks, died on Burgh Marsh on 7 July 1397 - see page 21.

He was known as the 'Hammer of the Scots' but his original plan was not to hammer them but plans tend to go wrong. The story starts with King Alexander III of Scotland who was crowned King of Scotland in 1249 at the age of seven years. During his minority the country was under the control of his second cousin - Robert de Brus, the 5th Lord Annandale - who reigned as Regent. Before Edward-I was crowned he and his brother went on a crusade with The 5th Lord of Annandale - Robert de Brus - and they became great friends. Robert was appointed Constable of Carlisle Castle.

In 1296, when Edward was king of England, he fought alongside Robert de Brus, the 6th Lord of Annandale at the Battle of Dunbar and reinforced the friendship between Edward and the Brus family. However, the friendship ended with Robert's son, the 7th Lord Annandale. He was Robert The Bruce who, inspired by a spider, later became King of Scotland.

Alexander III died in 1286 outliving his two sons, Alexander and David, and daughter Margaret. His first wife, Margaret daughter of the English King Henry III, died in 1275 so Alexander married Yolande of Dreux, France in 1285 in order to secure a male heir. Unfortunately he died before she could do so and he made his granddaughter, (Margaret's daughter also named Margaret), his heir. Thus Margaret, the Maid of Norway, became Queen of Scotland. This rather complex genealogy is clarified on the chart on the facing page which also shows Robert the Bruce's claim to the Scottish throne.

Margaret, (Maid of Norway), became Queen of Scotland in 1286 at the tender age of 3 years whilst she was living with her father, King Eric II of Norway. Edward Longshanks had 'a cunning plan'. He would marry his son Edward to Margaret and secure the kingdoms of England and Scotland. Unfortunately, Margaret died at the age of 7 years off Orkney whilst travelling from Norway to Scotland for her coronation.

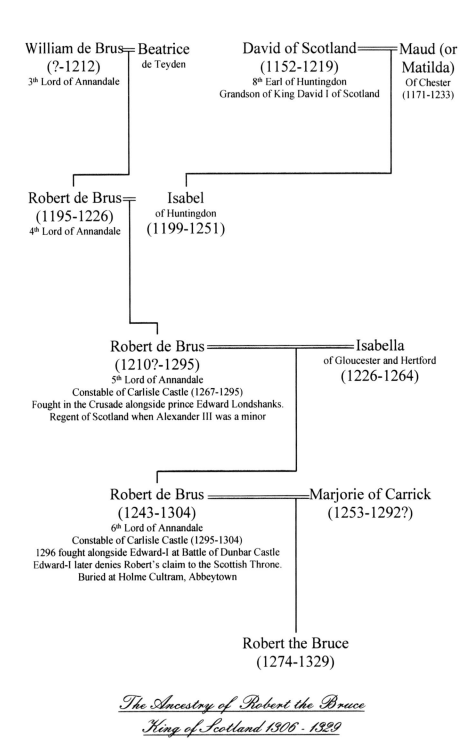

William de Brus
(?-1212)
3ᵗʰ Lord of Annandale

Beatrice
de Teyden

David of Scotland
(1152-1219)
8ᵗʰ Earl of Huntingdon
Grandson of King David I of Scotland

Maud (or Matilda)
Of Chester
(1171-1233)

Robert de Brus
(1195-1226)
4ᵗʰ Lord of Annandale

Isabel
of Huntingdon
(1199-1251)

Robert de Brus
(1210?-1295)
5ᵗʰ Lord of Annandale
Constable of Carlisle Castle (1267-1295)
Fought in the Crusade alongside prince Edward Londshanks.
Regent of Scotland when Alexander III was a minor

Isabella
of Gloucester and Hertford
(1226-1264)

Robert de Brus
(1243-1304)
6ᵗʰ Lord of Annandale
Constable of Carlisle Castle (1295-1304)
1296 fought alongside Edward-I at Battle of Dunbar Castle
Edward-I later denies Robert's claim to the Scottish Throne.
Buried at Holme Cultram, Abbeytown

Marjorie of Carrick
(1253-1292?)

Robert the Bruce
(1274-1329)

The Ancestry of Robert the Bruce
King of Scotland 1306 - 1329

In the ten years that span the change from 13th to 14th century, Edward I faced many rebellions in Scotland in which country he was considered its overlord. The final straw came when in 1306, Robert the Bruce was crowned King of an independent Scotland. In March 1307, Edward summoned his Parliament to meet in Carlisle having postponed a similar summons in the previous January due to the King's poor health.

The 68-year old king was too ill to ride on horseback and was carried on a horse litter which consisted of a seat supported by two poles mounted on either side of two horses, one horse at the front and other at the rear. No doubt such a means of transport avoided pot holes in the poorly maintained roads, but the sick king could only manage to travel a few miles each day. He based his headquarters in Lanercost Priory, near Brampton whilst some of his armies were engaged in Scotland but eventually decided to lead his army.

The 93 Bus retraces his final journey, but fortunately for today's passengers at a faster pace.

Carlisle: 26th June 1307.

Kirkandrews on Eden: 2nd July 1307.

Burgh by Sands: 5th July 1307 when he took to his bed and died at mid-day on 7th July 1307. His body lay in rest in St. Michael's Church, Burgh (see page 92) and was visited by his son, Edward, Prince of Wales, who had been in Scotland with the English Army at the time of his father's death. Edward II was crowned King of England in Carlisle on 8th July 1307. The body of Edward I was later taken to London where it was buried in Westminster Abbey.

In 1685 the Duke of Norfolk placed an obelisk on the site of Edward-I's death but this was replaced by a red sandstone monument that was erected in 1803 by the Earl of Lonsdale. Directions on how to walk to the monument are given on page 56.

As well as the charts on the opposite page and the one on the next page, please turn to page 21 to follow the ancestry of Edward-I.

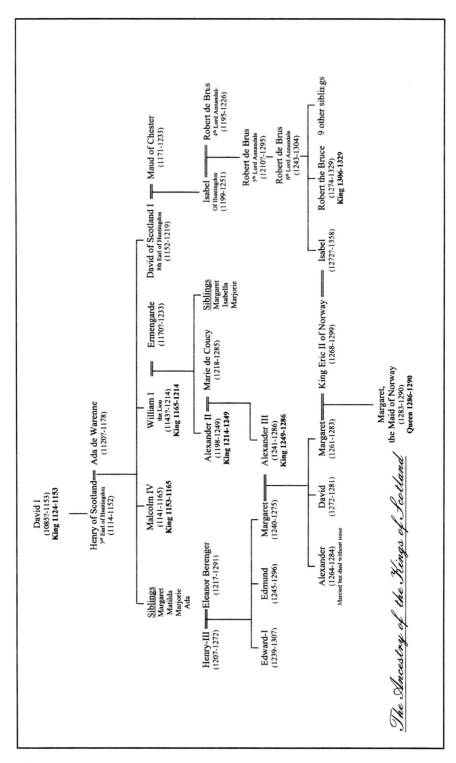

The Ancestry of the Kings of Scotland

David I
(1085?-1153)
King 1124-1153

Henry of Scotland
3rd Earl of Huntingdon
(1114-1152)
Ada de Warenne
(1120?-1178)

Siblings
Margaret
Matilda
Marjorie
Ada

Malcolm IV
(1141-1165)
King 1153-1165

William I
the Lion
(1143?-1214)
King 1165-1214
Ermengarde
(1170?-1233)

David of Scotland I
8th Earl of Huntingdon
(1152-1219)
Maud of Chester
(1171-1233)

Alexander II
(1198-1249)
King 1214-1249
Marie de Coucy
(1218-1285)

Siblings
Margaret
Isabella
Marjorie

Isabel
Of Huntingdon
(1199-1251)
Robert de Brus
4th Lord Annandale
(1195-1226)

Henry-III
(1207-1272)
Eleanor Berenger
(1217-1291)

Alexander III
(1241-1286)
King 1249-1286

Margaret
(1240-1275)

King Eric II of Norway
(1268-1299)
Margaret
(1261-1283)

Robert de Brus
5th Lord Annandale
(1210?-1295)

Isabel
(1272?-1358)

Edward-I
(1239-1307)

Edmund
(1245-1296)

Alexander
(1264-1284)
Married but died without issue

David
(1272-1281)

Margaret,
the Maid of Norway
(1283-1290)
Queen 1286-1290

Robert de Brus
6th Lord Annandale
(1243-1304)

Robert the Bruce
(1274-1329)
King 1306-1329

9 other siblings

Linking Carlisle to the Sea

Travel across land was difficult in the middle ages. The Romans had left Britain with a legacy of fine roads, but many of these had fallen into disrepair. Visitors to Carlisle had hills to climb, particularly Shap Summit. A few years ago an elderly neighbour of mine recalled how, as a project engineer, he had to bring a large copper vessel for Carlisle Brewery over Shap using a steam-powered lorry. It took over a week! Because of the Shap Barrier, Carlisle depended on the sea to transport people and Goods. In the middle ages the port was near Beaumont at a place called 'Sandsfield', but no evidence of it can be seen today. Walk 6, described on page 56, will take you to its location. Vessels of up to 60 tons brought timber, flax, tar, rice and general goods to the city and enabled the export of wheat, butter and alabaster.

When the Eden estuary on the Solway silted up and prevented large vessels from using Sandsfield, the Georgians decided to build a new port nearer the entrance of the Solway. They chose a place called Fisher's Cross and when they had built a large village there, they renamed it Port Carlisle. It was linked to the city of Carlisle by a canal.

The Carlisle Navigation Canal opened in 1823. It ran for 11¼ miles (18.1 km) mostly straight but made a dramatic sweep towards the Solway to the east of Drumburgh to avoid the higher ground on which the Romans used for their fort.

The canal's fortunes peaked in 1847 when steamers regularly ran to Liverpool, Whitehaven and the Isle of Man but by 1852 revenue had dropped to £3,600, one-third of its peak value causing the directors to consider draining the canal and replacing it with a railway. The Port Carlisle Dock and Railway Act was passed by parliament and received Royal Assent on 4 August 1853.

Six locks in a distance of 1¼ miles (2km) proved a challenge for the railway engineers and made the gradient of the railway somewhat higher and the curves were slightly more acute, than a traditional railway.

The Port Carlisle Line

The railway line to replace the canal was first conceived in 1847. Construction costs could be kept low by using the canal bed except between Kirkandrews and Beaumont where an embankment was built to avoid low lying ground just north of the Kirkandrews station. This can be seen from the bus between Kirkkandrews and Beamount (you may need to sit at the back of the bus where the seats are higher from the road) - see page 10.

In anticipation of the act, the canal was closed on 1st August and the new railway opened for goods traffic on 22 May 1854 with the first twelve passengers being carried from Carlisle on the morning of 22 June of that year. Later that day fifty passengers travelled on the afternoon train.

Initially the Newcastle and Carlisle Railway Company, some directors of which were also directors of the Port Carlisle Dock and Railway Company (PCDRC), provided a single locomotive/train, which started from the old canal basin (now the Port Road Business Park by the Jovial Sailor). The PCDRC acquired its own tank engine in 1855 and the following year a locomotive with tender.

At Drumburgh Station, the line split. One branch going to Port Carlisle and the other branch connecting to Silloth through Kirkbride

Burgh Railway Station
(early 20th century)

Drumburgh Railway Station
(early 20th century)

and Abbeytown. The harbour at Silloth was better for shipping to navigate than Port Carlisle and consequently more traffic used the Silloth branch than the Port Carlisle one.

Consequently in 1856 steam trains were replaced by a horse drawn carriage for passengers between Drumburgh and Port Carlisle. A single platform at Glasson provided access to passengers on this branch line. Some freight was still carried by steam locos.

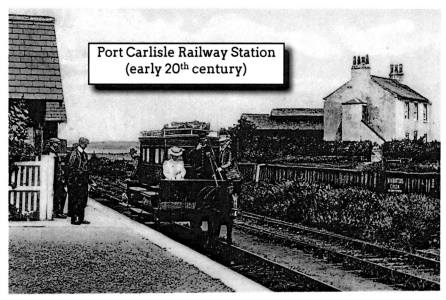

Port Carlisle Railway Station
(early 20th century)

In 1859 the first coach was replaced by *The Dandy* a four-wheeled vehicle based on the design of a stagecoach. It can be seen today at the National Railway Museum in York and had accommodation for three classes of passenger. If too many people arrived from Carlisle at Drumburgh Station, then *The Dandy* had to make several journeys to convey them all to Port Carlisle.

The Dandy at
Port Carlisle Railway Station
(early 20th century)

Work began to refurbish the track, which had become dangerous for steam locomotives, so that both freight and passengers could be carried.

The first train ceremoniously arrived at Port Carlisle on 6th April 1914 and was captured on the above picture. As a special 'Thank You' the horses that hauled the Dandy in years past got a lift in the van behind the engine.

In an attempt to reduce the cost of carrying passengers, a railcar known as *Flower of Yarrow* began in service in 1929 but low passenger numbers forced a closure of the line on 31 May 1932.

Carlisle, Kirkbride and Silloth Line

The Carlisle and Silloth Bay Railway opened in 1856. It ran between Carlisle and Drumburgh along the same track as the Port Carlisle Dock and Railway Company. Walkers on the Drumburgh Moss Nature Reserve (see page 68) walk alongside the path of the dismantled railway as far as Moss Cottage. The next stations after Kirkbride were Abbeyholme, Abbeytown, and Blackdyke before reaching the terminus in Silloth. The Port Carlisle Dock and Silloth Bay Railway Companies worked together to

More information (including a picture) of the *Flower of Yarrow* can be found at:

http://www.cumbria-railways.co.uk/port-carlisle-railway-yarrow.html

their mutual benefit but both faced financial difficulties that were solved to a certain extent by the North British Railway (NBR) who operated the Waverley Line between Edinbugh and Carlisle. The NBR was blocked from entering the Citadel Station by the other railway companies. They solved the problem by teaming up with the Silloth and Port Carlisle lines and used their station in what is now the Port Road Business Park (next to the Jovial Sailor see page 10). Goods from Edinburgh thus travelled down the Waverley Line to Carlisle, then through Drumburgh to Silloth where they were put on ships for destinations throughout England and Ireland. Passenger traffic was encouraged as well as freight and the NBR improved Silloth as a holiday resort, which became the playground of Carlisle.

In 1845 a rival railway company linked Carlisle with the sea. This one ran from Carlisle, through Dalston, Wigton. Aspatria and terminated on the coast at Maryport. Another factor in the demise of the railway was that in 1879 the NBR teamed up with the Midland Railway, which carried goods over the Settle line to the rest of England. Silloth lost its strategic importance for goods traffic and eventually the line closed.

Kirkbride Railway Station
(early 20th century)

The Solway Junction Railway

Iron ore mined in West Cumbria had a ready market in Lanarkshire and Ayreshire. To satisfy this need the the Caledonian Railway, built a line from its station in Kirtlebridge, through Annan. It built the Solway Viaduct across the Solway linking Annan with the stations at Bowness-on-Solway and Whitrigg.

The Viaduct was opened in 1869 after taking three years and about £100,000 to build. It spans 5,790 feet (1.76km). In 1875 and 1881 the climate was such that ice flows appeared on the Solway, which damaged the viaduct. Although these were repaired, the viaduct was demolished in 1934. The embankment on which it stood is now in a dangerous condition, (and is also private property), so nobody should walk there. The road was carried over a bridge (now demolished) and on the opposite side of the road is the old station (now a private dwelling). The late Sylvia Thompson told me how she got on the train at Bowness Station to go to school in Annan and at high tide water would splash into the carriages. Other people used the viaduct to walk between Annan and Bowness on Sundays when the public houses were closed in Scotland but open in England. It is not recorded how many fell into the Solway on their way home.

Bowness Railway Station
(early 20th century)

Another station was located at Whitrigg. The road climbs over a small embankment where the track was. A large house records the name of Whitrigg Station proudly on its gates. However, the house was built only a few years ago on the site and is completely unlike the old station.

A smaller viaduct carried the line at Whitrigg across the river Wampool /Moricambe Bay and into Kirkbride. It did not pass through Kirkbride station, but ran over the North British Railway track as far as Abbeytown, then joined the Maryport and Carlisle Railway at Brayton.

The line closed for passengers in 1914 and for freight in 1921.

The Victorian engineers ruined part of the Bowness Common peat bog and Natural England have been unable to restore it to its pristine condition. If such a project were contemplated today, a risk assessment of the damage to the environment would be carried out and ways of reducing or eliminating the damage engineered into the project. We can not stand in the way of progress but many projects today have shown that we can 'have our cake and eat it'.

Inspired by the Solway Viaduct many people have thought of building a new structure in its place to harness the tide. However, this would have a damaging effect on marine life. The dream now is to make lagoons along the Solway that would cause minimum environmental disturbance and still harnessing tidal power.

Part 4- Eco-Tourism

visiting the many nature reserves on the bus route

Two important nature reserves are just off the bus route and are therefore beyond the scope of this book. However information on these can be found on the Internet at the following websites:

Wedholme Flow is the largest of the South Solway Mosses Nature Reserves and is located between Kirkbride and Wigton. http://solwaywetlands.org.uk/weird-and-wonderful-wedholme

The Watchtree Nature Reserve is located about three miles south of Kirkbampton and was created after the Foot and Mouth Disease livestock burial site was closed to ensure that nobody will disturb the animal graves. http://www.watchtree.co.uk/

Drumburgh Moss NNR

Drumburgh Moss National Nature Reserve is a site of international importance, dominated by an expanse of lowland raised mire. Sphagnum moss, sundew and other bog-loving plants thrive in the wetlands that make up much of the terrain. Curlew and red grouse breed and adders and roe deer are seen.

The best time to visit this 121 hectare site is between April and August. There is a level and usually dry path to the viewing platform that offers fantastic views across the mire and to the hills beyond. Wellington boots are required for other paths which can be very wet and uneven. There are also adders and ticks present on the site.

Sphagnum is not the only plant to be found. Drumburgh moss is home to a number of specialist bog plants. In spring, the moss is a profusion of the white heads of cotton grass, dancing in the wind. In summer cranberry, bog rosemary and later heather are in flower. You can find all three species of sundew here including the scarce great sundew. Sundews have adapted to low nutrients of the bog by trapping and digesting flies on sticky filaments on their leaves.

In spring you might be treated to breeding displays of curlew, skylark and reed buntings. Red grouse, redshank, snipe and grasshopper warbler also breed here. Autumn is a good time to spot short-eared owls quartering the moss. The nationally rare large heath butterfly is on the wing from June to August looking for cotton grass on which it lays its eggs. The pools near the nature reserve entrance are alive with dragonflies and damselflies during the summer months. In winter the nature reserve often hosts small numbers of geese from the huge flocks on the Solway.

Summer is the time to find adders and common lizards basking. At all times of year you might catch a glimpse of the shy roe deer and hares or perhaps a fox.

Around the moss are areas of wet and dry heath, scrub and grassland which are managed by grazing. Long horn cattle and hardy Exmoor ponies are used to keep the vegetation open.

The site is managed by the Cumbria Wildlife Trust, who have kindly provided the above information. For more information please visit their website at: http://www.cumbriawildlifetrust.org.uk

In 1857 a chemical works was built on Drumbugh Moss at Whiteholme to make sulphuric and other acids used in the distillation of tar.

Glasson Moss NNR

Walk 14 (see page 72) passes the entrance to the Caravan Park. A continuation of the footpath leads to the nature reserve. The walk is flat and easy going with wooden boardwalks over the boggy parts of the moss

Glasson Moss is one of the South Solway Mosses managed by Natural England (the others are Bowness Common and Wedholme Flow). Forestry, agriculture and commercial peat extraction have reduced the 95 thousand hectares of Britain's peatbogs to 6 thousand hectares and most of these (1.9 thousand hectares) are along this bus route. Drumburgh Moss is also one of these raised mires but is maintained by Cumbria Wildlife Trust, whilst management of Bowness Common is split between the RSPB and Natural England.

The bogs are higher in their centre than around their edges - hence the term 'raised bog'. The vegetation on the bogs can not get nutrients from the soil because soil has not formed. Instead they absorb nutrients from the atmosphere and the sundew is a carnivorous plant living on flies. Trees, known as the lagg zone, surround the bog. These provide a perch for birds whose droppings provide nutrients for other plants and thus the process of soil formation starts.

About a metre below the surface the pollen embedded in the peat changes from tree pollen to the pollen from arable crops and weeds marking the time when the Roman's deforested this area to build Hadrian's Wall and the other fortifications and buildings. After the Romans left, natural forces restored the habitat. Pools that formed between 400 and 800 AD were used on Glasson Moss in medieval times for hemp retting. In this process the harvested hemp was placed in these ponds and held down with stones for about ten days in order to allow microbes to separate the fibre. It is thought that Glasson Hemp was then made into rope and sails for shipping, but these ships would be sailing from Sandsfield as Port Carlisle did not exist then.

Bowness Nature Reserve

The bus will stop outside the entrance upon request. Alternatively, the reserve is only a walk of about 20 minutes from Bowness. A farm track splits this nature reserve in two. The Cumbria Wildlife Trust has provided some seating along a way-marked path around this delightful small reserve, which features butterflies, moths, dragonflies, wildflowers and of course birds such as the willow tit. See http://www.cumbriawildlifetrust.org.uk/

Campfield Marsh

The RSPB manage the reserve that is made up of a mosaic of salt-marsh, peat-bogs, farmland and wet grassland providing homes for a great variety of native wildlife. Trails lead to a wheelchair accessible hide looking out over the main wet grassland area where lapwings, redshanks and snipe breed in the summer and thousands of swans, ducks and geese spend the winter.

Longer trails over more difficult terrain cross the peat-bog where bog plants and dragonflies abound.

Reserve open at all times. Visitor centre open 10 am to 4 pm most days and manned at weekends. Entry is free but donations to help maintain the reserve are welcome.

More information is available on the RSPB website at:

http://www.rspb.org.uk/discoverandenjoynature/seenature/reserves/guide/c/campfieldmarsh/about.aspx

Rogersceugh

The RSPB acquired Rogersceugh Farm in 2004 and added it to its Campfield Reserve. Now it is possible to walk from the West Common bus stop, across both Campfield and Rogersceugh and catch the bus at the Longcroft bus stop (or vice versa) - see Walk 17 on page 80.

Rogersceugh is built on a hill that was created by glacial deposits (known as a drumlin) and as such provides a panoramic view of the Bowness Peninsular.

Bowness Common - Cardurnock Moss

Walk 18 on page 78 describes how to reach Cardurnock Moss, which is part of the much larger Bowness Common. A heron is sometimes seen in the ponds and pools alongside the track and owls used to nest in the shooting on the airfield, although I have not seen them recently. In the Spring I once caught sight of a female cockoo in one of the trees alongside the lonning.

Raised bogs of this quality are rare in the UK and Natural England, who manage the site, have dug ponds recently to conserve this Site of Special Scientific Importance (SSSI).

Near the end of the lonning you may find a clump of daffodils. These have escaped from a nearby cottage garden. The cottage was a ruin when we first moved here in the 1970's and subsequently its building materials have been removed as rubble for use eleswhere by the farming community. The site is now underwater as part of the conservation project and all that is left is the daffodils that return each year. I don't know who lived there, but I am touched that even after all traces of them have disappeared their love remains, symbolised by the daffodils.

At the end of the lonning is an information board standing next to

a pond. Over the years I have watched as the pond has changed from a clear pool enjoyed by the wild ducks, to being gradually filled in by the sphagnum moss. Eventually, the moss will absorb all the water and solidify the ground - this is evolution in action. The cotton grass (eriophorum), shown here on the left, is spectacular on Cardurnock Moss.

Finglandrigg Wood

This is my favourite nature reserve and provides access for wheelchair users along good paths and boardwalks enabling the disabled to reach far into the reserve. The site, managed by Natural England, is one of the largest areas of semi-

natural woodland on the Solway Plain and provides habitat for

red squirrels and roe deer as well as a range of wild flowers. Badgers can not be seen during the day, but their setts are evidence that they live here. Over 40 species of breeding birds have been recorded in Finglandrigg Wood including buzzard, tawny owl, reed bunting and long-tailed tit.

A chalybeate well, i.e. a well that provides mineral spring waters containing salts of iron, is a feature of one of the paths. Tunbridge Wells owes its fame and fortune to a its own chalybeate well but I am not sure how widespread the knowledge of the Finglandrigg well was known beyond the immediate parish.

Cardurnock Marsh

This is not a nature reserve, but a marsh warden is responsible for ensuring the area is safe, especially for the sheep and cattle that graze there.

It can be difficult for the inexperienced to walk on the marsh due to the route being blocked by inlets and ponds and there are quicksands further out. Furthermore, walking in the marsh may disturb the very birds that the visitor wants to see. Therefore, it is recommended to walk along the road between Cardurnock and Anthorn which provides a better viewpoint for the wildlife.

During Autumn, Winter and into Spring, Barnacle Geese can be seen grazing in the fields, particularly on the Solway side of the road. The flock runs into hundreds and if they take off overhead - the sky turns black with their number. It is an impressive sight/sound and well worth the 3-mile walk between bus stops in Cardurnock and Anthorn.

In the summer such a walk is accompanied by the sound of the Skylark. Other birds favour this area as well : golden plover, lapwing (peewit), whooper swans, pink-footed geese, white-fronted geese, grey heron, great white egret, oyster catcher, gulls, shoveler, ringed plover and even a spoonbill has been spotted. Many people use telescopes to get the best pictures, but the modern digital camera with inbuilt zoom is capable of getting excellent results. Rest your elbow on one of the many fencing posts to avoid hand shake. I often take a sequence of several pictures in quick succession to offset problems of handshake and afterwards select the best of the sequence.

Part 5 Miscellany

Beware The Tides On Marsh

Spring tides occur twice every month at new moon and full moon. At these times the road floods at Anthorn and along the Burgh Marsh and it is dangerous to walk on the coastal marshes. For this reason the area is sometimes referred to as 'The Island' although in reality the side roads linking the coast to the Kirkbride-Carlisle road provide an alternative route.

When a tide is predicted to be more than 9 metres, the road will tend to flood in these places. With a strong on-shore wind the predicted tide height will be much higher. As a rule of thumb the high tides occur three or four days either side of new and full moon between 11 and 5 o-clock Am and PM but more detailed forecasts are available from the website: http://www.tidetimes.co.uk/silloth-tide-times. Please bear in mind that it can take a hour for the tide to peak in Burgh after it has done so in Silloth and you should not venture onto the marsh during the one hour before and after high tide.

Quicksands are a danger even at low tide and although the beaches look tempting visitors should consult experienced locals before walking there.

The Solway coast is a very gently sloping gradient whereby tidal energy is dissipated before reaching habitation. Unlike the east coast where cliffs take the full energy of the tide and coastal erosion threatens the houses near the cliff edge. The down side of this is that the Solway tide comes in VERY QUICKLY and a few inches rise in sea level is translated into several yards on the ground. At such times it is impossible to out-run the tide and unfortunately some people have lost their lives though carelessly ignoring such warnings. Neverthless, at all other times, the salt-marsh provides a wonderful place to walk. Dogs owners should be aware that farm animals also share the marsh and they, together with wild birds, should not be disturbed.

CPSIA information can be obtained
at www.ICGtesting.com
Printed in the USA
LVOW07s1714260617

539414LV00013B/1082/P

9 781537 177199